Sent to Prison:

A Chaplain's Story

Kathey McCollum

Sent to Prison
A Chaplain's Story
Copyright © 2021 by Gwendolyn Irene, LLC
Published by Amazon KDP
Tulsa, OK
www.gwendolynirene.com
www.betterlifefamilyministries.com

Printed in the United States of America

About

Chaplain Kathryn McCollum declares that she went into prison to find inmates. Instead, she found women: Broken Women; Desperate Women; Weary Women; Emotionally Worn Women.

Have you ever wondered what a woman who is incarcerated has at her disposal to better improve her life?

Does God *really* make THE difference in an inmate's life?

Is it just "jailhouse religion"? Or does lasting change *really* happen as a result of giving one's life to Christ?

What can inmates do for their children and themselves *while* they are incarcerated?

As a Chaplain for 22 years at Eddie Warrior Correctional Center, an 800- female minimum-security facility; armed with a Master's Degree in Biblical Studies and a direct call to prison ministry, Chaplain McCollum implemented and taught effective faith-based and non faith-based programs from initial incarceration, to the aftercare process with an emphasis on female offenders relationships with their children and others. She managed the 53 church groups that came into adjunct church services, and the 600 volunteers who faithfully visited to lead services, classes and make programs happen.

Many inmates' callings were birthed at EWCC. Church services exploded so much so that they had to turn inmates away. Each class offered had long waiting lists of 350 inmates or more.

Undeniable recorded miracles, healings and deliverances took place at EWCC.

Chaplain McCollum believes in the power of God to change lives, applying the principle that mercy and truth work together as minds are daily/continually renewed by the Word of God. She truly believes that Jesus came to heal the brokenhearted and bind up their wounds. What better place to show Himself strong to women who are broken and wounded than in prison?

The Presence of God was tangible at Eddie Warrior Correctional Center. He came because they welcomed Him; He stayed because we worshipped Him. We worshipped with our lives, teachings and examples of excellence.

Dedication

This book is dedicated to the incarcerated women who fought so valiantly to love and trust the LIGHT, and who were subsequently translated out of the kingdom of darkness, into the Kingdom of His Dear Son *and* the dedicated, compassionate, faithful volunteers who helped them get there.

I also dedicate this book to every Chaplain who serves at a correctional facility, no matter what security level. They work hard and strive for innovative ways to make God known to the inmates they serve. They not only do everything they can to bring in the Light, but they strive to be an extension of that Light in the darkness of their respective prisons. And they do it with integrity, spiritual strength, and the Love of God.

I want to thank my husband, Bobby. He was my biggest fan and I miss him every day. My children, Jeff, Gwen, and Mandy, and my grandsons, Thomas, Nathan, and Alex have always been so supportive and encouraging during the 22 years I served as a Chaplain, *and* they cheered me on in writing this book. Their love strengthened me.

Kathey

Acknowledgements

I have ministered at Eddie Warrior Correctional Center Chapel several times. Our church, Victory Christian Center in Tulsa, Oklahoma, has Bible Colleges in prisons around the state and in other states in the United States.

Eddie Warrior is so different from other correctional centers because Chaplain Kathey McCollum has allowed the Lord to minister to the women there. Eddie Warrior is like a family of women who believe God can change their lives. They worship God with sincere passion. They learn what the God-kind of love is; not the world's perverted love. They truly care for each other and want to see each other go forward with their lives. They pray and believe for miracles in the lives of one another and they've seen those miracles manifest. They encourage each other and they are serious about learning the Word of God. They look after each other.

They have learned how to forgive others and they've learned how to receive God's forgiveness for their own lives. By this, they've been healed of past hurts and past wrongs that they've done to others and harm done to themselves. When they are finished with the programs that Chaplain

Kathryn (McCollum) offers for consistency, they are new people, and they are ready to enter back into society. Chaplain gives them opportunity to go through various programs to set them free and heal them.

Eddie Warrior is the greatest example of a successful chapel program in a correctional center we have seen anywhere around the United States.

Pastor Sharon Daugherty, Victory Tulsa

Over the years, my wife and I have had the privilege of conducting services at Eddie Warrior Correctional Center in Taft, Oklahoma. I'll never forget the first time we arrived at the Chapel. We were stunned to see 200 born-again, spirit-filled women in the Chapel worshipping God with all their hearts.

We came to minister to the inmates, but their love and zeal were ministering to us! The women themselves had organized the music, a drama and the praise and worship. Chaplain McCollum is a visionary whom God has used to create one of the most successful prison ministries we have ever encountered.

Not only has Chaplain McCollum created an amazing curriculum for the women inmates to get help while they are at Eddie Warrior, but she also has made classes available that are designated to help families still at home with children and codependent issues. Nothing shocks Chaplain McCollum. She has a gift for straight-ahead teaching that deals with abuse, addictions and wrong choices that put these women into incarceration, placing before them alternative life choices to rebuild their lives so they will not return to prison after release.

Eddie Warrior Correctional Center had no funding available for a designated Chapel building with classrooms and all the amenities of a real church building. So Chaplain McCollum reached out to churches and individuals everywhere. She received permission from the authorities and raised funds to build a fully functional facility Chapel inside the fence on the grounds of the Center wholly on donations: with no state funds!

Thousands of lives are being radically changed by the faith and wisdom of this amazing woman.

Len and Cathy Mink Ministries

In November 2012, I was appointed Warden at Eddie Warrior Correctional Center. That began God's revealed mission for me. I knew this was where God had intended for me to serve Him in a mighty way.

That's when I met this awesome woman of God; a woman of excellence, a true child of God, Kathryn McCollum. Chaplain McCollum was a servant of God and God had put us together to bring about a spiritual change; a change that was so desperately needed, not only for the inmates but for the staff as well.

The programs and services provided by Chaplain McCollum and her volunteers were so inspiring. It brought light to a very dark place. The Chapel Program began to blossom into a safe haven, a place of peace and love to so many broken and lost women; those that lost hope, those that had faith, but felt as though they had lost faith; and those that did not know God for the awesome God He is. He is truly worthy to be praised. Due to the wonderful programs that Chaplain McCollum added, she helped change so many lives. Women were discharged ready for a new life, a better life, healed from their brokenness, pain and sorrow. Mothers, sisters, grandmothers, daughters—all ready to go back home to their families, to make their families proud, to mend broken relationships that seemed as though nothing could ever be done to mend those relationships. They would leave with hope and love in their hearts.

These programs helped the women to focus on themselves and work out their pain and suffering, the specific cause and effect of how they ended up incarcerated and mad at the world.

Programs like Play Day, Mom's Touch, the Praise Team, Inmate Christian Leaders, Christian Women's Association, Christmas, Easter, and Mother's Day plays, all of which built women's confidence, and motivated and encouraged women to push themselves to accomplish goals they never thought they could achieve and taught them how to take control of their lives through their Christian faith. They learned how to pray for a husband (a Boaz), and not a man with no character, and to recognize the difference between a husband and a man.

These programs and services had a great spiritual impact on these women. God truly heard the cry of His children.

Having a Christian Facility head Warden and a Christian Chaplain, which God used for His glory made for an unstoppable pair. Chaplain McCollum was definitely a great and powerful foot soldier, and I was hers as I followed her lead. Together, we were a great team that God set up so He would get the glory and we were truly honored that He chose us to do His will. Everything that we touched was good because He blessed it.

Warden Sharon McCoy,
Oklahoma Department of Corrections

Foreword

During my employment, Oklahoma had the highest percentage of women incarcerated than any other state in the United States. There are many things that the Oklahoma Department of Corrections and Chaplains try to do—but THERE ARE SO MANY THINGS THAT ONLY GOD CAN DO.

I hope that this book enlightens, inspires, and states clearly and candidly, what I have experienced working with the incarcerated women I have had the privilege of serving for over 22 years. If it seems that the book flips quickly back and forth between laughter and mourning, it's because that is really how the atmosphere was at Eddie Warrior Correctional Center.

I have only included a few actual names in my "stories," because I don't want to leave any volunteer or incarcerated woman out. I have had the privilege of serving *with* so many wonderful volunteers *and* inmates that I have met over the years. So, I have changed names and certain details of every story to *protect the innocent and the guilty!!*

Content

CHAPTER 1

Sent to Prison

**"In Him was the Life and the Life was
the Light of men, And the Light shines
on in the darkness and the darkness has
never overpowered it..."**
John 1:4,5 (AMP)

**"Life came into being because of Him,
for His Life is Light for all humanity,
and this Living Expression is the Light
that bursts through the gloom;
the Light that darkness could not
diminish."**
John 1:4,5 (TPT)

**"What came into existence was Life and
the Life was Light to live by. The Life-
Light blazed out of the darkness and the
darkness could not put it out."**
John 1:5 (Message)

Everything was gray. I felt so alone and truly afraid.
How did I end up in prison? It all happened so fast, and yet,
it seemed it had been in the works for a long time.

I was interrupted by a commanding male voice that startled me out of my reflective thoughts. "Chaplain, I'm the Chief of Security here at Eddie Warrior. Let me know if there is ever anything you need." He looked around and said evenly, "So, they've got you down here?"

"Yes," I replied. He looked around again, then he left.

"Down here" was the basement of the gym. It was damp, and when it rained, it held about one to two inches of water that I had to slog through to get out of my office. I often said we had the most spiritual termites in the world – they literally ate the meager store of Bibles and religious books I had stashed in the damp storage closet down here. My office and a semi-large classroom were here.

It really was a dreary spot, but I could not have been happier. I just didn't understand WHY I was so happy. But then, I really *did* know why the damp basement didn't bother me: *God* had placed me here.

My thoughts about the reality of my being in a prison setting seeped back into my mind. *How did it all happen?*

Several years prior to this my husband Bobby, my greatest encourager and fan, was licensed and ordained with a particular church organization, [and] I, too, was invited by the organization to be licensed and ordained. I was excited! We had done evangelistic ministry, but God had opened a door that we both wanted to walk through: My husband was pastor of a church.

To my surprise, when I mentioned I was looking forward to both of us being licensed and ordained, my husband said, "Kathey, I'm not going to let you be licensed and ordained with me."

"Why not?" I snapped back. I was immediately defensive and not just a little angry. After all, I felt I had been supportive of Bobby in every move towards the ministry calling on *his* life. Why was I left out now? In an even and firm tone, but with love behind it, he stated, "Kathey, you have been an obedient 'helpmeet' to me, but you have your own ministry calling and you need to know what that is. I want to put you on as an Associate Pastor for

3

the next *two years*. You will have to do as others have done and work, not just as my wife, but as someone on staff. And you need to seek the Lord intensely and be more serious about your personal calling."

Well, being told what to do is not my strong suit. Especially, since it was my husband telling me what to do. I immediately blurted out, "That sounds unfair and hard; and besides, don't I get any points for being intimate with the Pastor?" I laughed. Bobby didn't. He said, "No, you don't—*and* that mouth of yours is one of the things you need to work on!" I'm still working on that one, even *now*. I really was mad, but strangely, I felt a peace about this down deep inside and I knew what Bobby was saying *was* really GOD. I knew I would pout for a while, but that I would do this because my husband Bobby always heard from God and had the courage to state unapologetically what he had heard from Him.

For *two years*, I did what Bobby, as a pastor, asked me to do (a fate worse than death), but more important I did follow my husband's spiritual instructions: I sought the Lord.

After two years as Associate Pastor, I walked into my husband's (Pastor Bob's) office and stated that I thought I had cleaned just about enough toilets to be licensed and ordained now. Bobby said, "Yes, you are ready to be licensed and ordained—not because you cleaned toilets, but because you have really sought the Lord. Remember, Kathey, you have been an obedient helpmeet to me, but you have your own ministry calling and you need to know that." Bobby spoke this same statement to me several times during the course of those two years. I felt strangely unsure and, yet, very sure of myself every time he did.

When the time came for me to take part in my ordination, a group of about 100 other ministers were to be ordained also. I was surprised when Bobby said that he was NOT going to go to the ordination with me. He said I would have to do it on my own.

That Saturday night before my ordination the next morning, I was praying in the church we pastored. It was totally dark in the sanctuary, and I suddenly heard very distinctly a strong, clear voice say, "You will go into women's prison, and that will be your great harvest." Tears came to my eyes, grateful towards God for speaking to me, yet I had never stepped foot in a prison before and I could hardly believe what I had heard. For just a minute afterwards, I wondered if God had the wrong number, or we had a bad connection. It was just so far out there for me.

The next morning, I shared with Bobby what the Lord had spoken to me. The look on his face was priceless: he asked if I was sure that was God? He said, "After all, you have never liked working with people who had broken the law, or working with people with major drug problems, etc. Then he just stopped. I could tell he was trying to be positive but having a hard time absorbing what I felt the Lord said.

Sunday Ordination Morning. I listened to a sermon and was placed in a line with about 100 other people for the presiding minister and his wife to lay hands on all of us. They had gone down the line of prospective ministers, laid hands on each of us and prayed. But when they came to me, the wife had a "tongue" and her husband had the "interpretation". The interpretation that came out of his mouth was: "You have been an obedient helpmeet, but you have your own ministry, and you need to know it." *That* husband-and-wife team had never heard what Bobby had spoken to me, but the words that came out were exactly what

Bobby had quoted to me ---more than once. What a confirmation!

And, once that couple laid hands on me and prayed for me, I left with another benefit: Although I had operated in prophesy or had a Word from the Lord, from *that* time on, I could only prophesy in RHYME. In the natural, I couldn't rhyme "blow" and "go". I was never a poet or anything close to one, but:

> **"Do not neglect the gift which is in you, that special inward endowment which was directly imparted to you by the Holy Spirit by prophetic utterance when the elders laid their hands upon you at your ordination. Practice and cultivate and meditate upon these duties: throw yourself wholly into them as your ministry, so that your progress may be evident to everybody. Look well to yourself, to your own personality and to your teaching; persevere in these things; hold to them for by so doing you will save both yourself and those who hear you."**
>
> **I Timothy 4:14-16 (AMP)**

Shortly after my ordination, my husband was stricken with a horrible, painful disease in his legs and body. We believed God for his healing with all our might, but soon, we had to resign our church. Bobby was really ill and the church began to diminish.

For the next eight years, we struggled financially, physically and, at times, spiritually. Things got rougher, so we had to get tougher. Bobby got worse and I was working two jobs. During this time, I saw what my husband was *really* made of. In the most desperate of circumstances, I saw my husband stand, confess and declare the goodness and the healing power of God. I was not as faith filled as Bobby during these times. I felt like giving up, but Bobby kept believing God's Word and His promises of healing, restoration and prosperity. I admire him so much for his spiritual valor in those bad times.

Finally, after several years, we got a breakthrough. Bobby began to get better, and we began to experience the financial blessings of God, and, I had a good job. Our needs were being met and we were genuinely appreciative towards Jesus and His Word.

But a funny thing happened on the way to prosperity and relief: the Holy Spirit began to deal with me in a strong way. I had been teaching a little Bible study at lunchtime at work, but I knew this was not my real calling. Have you ever done something for God that was "Godly," but not really God's ultimate will for you?

Every morning on my way to work, the Holy Spirit would deal with me. and I felt His force in my heart. I began to pray in the Spirit and weep, every morning, on my way to work for the next five months.

> **"For one who speaks in an unknown tongue speaks not to men but to God for no one understands or catches His meaning, because in the Holy Spirit he utters secret truth and hidden things not obvious to the understanding."**
> **I Corinthians 14:2 (AMP)**

> **"And He who searches the hearts of men knows what is in the mind of the Holy Spirit, what His intent is, because the Spirit intercedes and pleads before God on behalf of the saints according to and in harmony with God's Will."**
> **Romans 8:27 (AMP)**

I didn't really understand what God wanted of me. To my shame, I have to say that I honestly didn't remember that eight years ago, the night before I was to be licensed and ordained, while praying God had spoken to me so miraculously "You will be going into a women's prison and that will be your great harvest." So much of life had happened.

Then I ran into someone I knew, who was a well-known prison minister. I had shared with her that I felt led to prison in some way I wasn't sure of. She said, "I can show you how to get into prison." I told her "Just don't forget to show me how to get out: I don't want to spend the night!" I'm really a sissy. She took me with her to her next prison service at Eddie Warrior Correctional Center. I spoke a little and just followed her lead, but my spirit was conflicted. I felt comfortable, if somewhat scared, but I didn't feel comfortable sharing the Word in the front of the women prisoners. When I spoke to her about this, she said maybe I was called to be a "Chaplain."

So, what does a Chaplain do? I thought. A few days later she called to tell me to go see the man who was currently Chaplain at Eddie Warrior Correctional Center: Leo Brown. She said, 'It's imperative that you go see him within the next few days.' I began to pray for clarity. Then I went to meet Chaplain Leo Brown. He was so kind. We talked for a while, and he asked me to come in as a volunteer.

I told him I would think and pray about it. By the time I made the drive home, I was ready to tell my husband, Bobby, that I felt led to quit my secular job and go to help Chaplain Leo Brown as a volunteer. My husband thought about this one for a while. After all, we were just seeing daylight in our finances and had recently been through many battles. But characteristic of the man I married, Bobby said, "Kathey, it's a little bit hard, but you have always supported me in my ministry endeavors, and I will support you in yours. You do what you feel you should do, and we'll do whatever we need to do."

A few days later, I went back to see Chaplain Brown. I told him of the decision my husband and I had made concerning my volunteering. He asked me about my education. Had I completed college? Did I have my master's degree in ministry? The answer to both questions was "no."

Then, Leo Brown informed me that he has been praying and asking God to transfer him to Jess Dunn Correctional Center, a men's correctional facility just a half-mile down the road from Eddie Warrior Correctional Center.

He said that he prayed that whoever replaced him at Eddie Warrior would do an even better job than he had done while he was at Eddie Warrior; but God sent me instead. That was characteristic of Leo Brown. He wanted the best for the inmates he had been Chaplain to. But to be a Chaplain with the Oklahoma Department of Corrections required a Master's Degree in Biblical Studies or something comparable.

He said that he had done some research and the Department of Corrections had a then obscure and rarely used job description that was "part-time temporary" and that, even though I did not have the necessary degrees to fill the Chaplaincy position, I could work part time for two years while I was getting my degree. I was surprised, delighted and... scared spitless.

Leo changed from the women's facility (EWCC) to the men's facility just half a mile down the road. After he left, I drove him nuts asking 100 questions per hour. I was soaking up everything he told me, then promptly forgot it all when he left. There I was: Chaplain at Eddie Warrior Correctional Center—a minimum security women's facility housing, at that time, about 550 inmates. Since then, we

12

have become an overcrowded facility of 800–900 incarcerated women.

Leo Brown was then, and has remained even to this day, someone I go to for advice and guidance as a Chaplain. As I muddled my way through being a Chaplain, Leo was promoted to Head Chaplain in the State of Oklahoma Department of Corrections, a well-deserved appointment. It's good to have friends in high places. Leo was, and still is, a good friend.

So, here I was in a gray world. Everything in the Department of Corrections was gray: gray walls; gray floors; gray trim; and gray uniforms for incarcerated individuals. I have never been so tired of any color in my life!

CHAPTER 2

My Degree

"In all your ways, know, recognize and acknowledge Him and He will direct and make straight and plain your paths."
Proverbs 3:6 (AMP)

I immediately began to try to figure out how to get my master's degree. Our Human Resources director said I could get it anywhere, as long as it was an "accredited" school where I could obtain a master's degree. A fellow Chaplain told me about a Bible College in the Oklahoma City area. He stated that they were great people and that he was sure they would work with me on getting my Master's in Biblical Studies, but he didn't think they were an accredited college.

I called this wonderful group of people, and they were a little taken back when I told them they had to be accredited for me to get my degree from them. A very nice lady on the phone paused for a moment, then said, "We have been trying for a while now to get our accreditation and we just got it four weeks ago."

For the next two years I worked more than I showed on my timesheet as a part -time employee as far as hours go – sometimes until 8:00 p.m., because there is no way you can completely do the job of a Chaplain without putting in lots and lots of hours, *and* I worked on my degree. I got my transcript from Tulsa University and the Bible college got everything squared away with me and I started correspondence learning. Not many Bible Colleges had a completely online curriculum at that time. Not only did the Bible College work *with* me, but they also worked *for* me. I really didn't know how we were going to pay for these college hours, but this wonderful school, knowing that I was a prison Chaplain, forgave me of so much tuition that I ended up paying about $1,200 for my *entire* Master's of Biblical Studies degree. The sad thing is that I heard they lost their accreditation about a year after I finished my degree. What a window of opportunity God had given me!

As a Chaplain for the State of Oklahoma, you are required to have a Master Degree in Biblical Studies or

Divinity, and you are required to have been in full-time ministry for at least two years. I worked as an Associate Pastor to my husband for exactly two years.

During the first few years I worked as a Chaplain, I answered to the Case Manager Supervisor at EWCC, Greg Breslin. He was my "boss" and was always kind and respectful to me—and he always made me laugh. I had been working this part-time, temporary job as Chaplain for Eddie Warrior Correctional Center for over two years. The money and time frame to be able to work part time had run out. I was going on my sixth month without a paycheck and was working at a store by my house stocking shelves on the weekend to help us financially. My wonderful husband was beginning to get a little concerned about our finances – and so was I.

At this time, I distinctly remember walking around the curve of the sidewalk that led from the Administration building. This building housed the Warden, Deputy Warden and Chief of Security, and was referred to as "The White House" by inmates. I said in my heart: "Lord, I appreciate all you have done for me, but You said in Your Word that a 'workman is worthy of his hire.' If I don't get hired on permanently, so that I can do the job and get paid for it full time, I will need to quit.

Two weeks later, we had a new Warden: Eric Franklin (one of my favorite Wardens). He asked my boss, Greg, what he thought the first thing he needed to do as a new Warden? My boss said that we needed to hire our part-time Chaplain, *full time*. And in three days, it was done. God is so good! And I am so thankful for God putting people like Greg Breslin and Warden Franklin in my life.

CHAPTER 3

My Office

Earlier I mentioned the damp, dark, office where I had been housed. It really *did* flood every time it rained. Years later, a French drain was dug, and it no longer flooded. I had this Office/Chapel for three years.

I didn't want to complain to God because I was so grateful to be doing what I was doing. But one day just before I left for the day, I opened the storage closet to get a Bible for an inmate and saw termites everywhere. It was raining and the water in the place we called "The Chapel" was starting to rise. I stood in the middle of the room I sighed, then said quietly to the Lord: "Lord I don't mean to complain, but could you please get me out of here to someplace else on the compound?" Then I just sighed again and waded towards my car.

Two weeks later, we had a new Deputy Warden. We went through Wardens, Deputy Wardens and Chiefs of Security on a regular basis. The Department of Corrections encourages people to try to better themselves within the facility they work in by applying for different positions. It's really a healthy way to employ people who work in Corrections. It encourages people to promote and to experience all aspects of Corrections work.

The Chief of Security at that time was showing the new Deputy Warden, where every department was located on the compound prison grounds. When Chief brought the new Deputy around, it had just rained. I introduced myself to the Deputy as we all stood in a good half-inch of water and he slowly looked back to my office area, then at the wet floor, and said, "So this is where we have our Chaplain?" "Well, yes" the Chief replied." Again, the new Deputy Warden said "Hmm, so this is where we have our Chaplain?" Then he ever-so-slightly shook his head. There was an awkward silence as this new Deputy looked around again.

Four days later, an officer came to my office and said "Chaplain, you need to pack up all the Chapel Stuff because we're moving your office to the Programs Building." I soon came to know that our new Deputy at that time was a dedicated Christian who expressed his disapproval of putting our Chaplain in a leaky basement, and that one of the first things he did as a Deputy was to move me out of the damp, dark area I had occupied for the last three years. I was so thankful to God and his obedient, caring servant.

CHAPTER 4

What Chaplains Do

"But arise and stand upon your feet: for
I have appeared to you for this purpose,
that I might appoint you to serve as My
minister and to bear witness both to
what you have seen of Me and to that in
which I will appear to you."
                    Acts 26:16 (AMP)

"Of this Gospel I was made a minister
according to the gift of God's free grace
and undeserved favor which was
bestowed on me by the exercise, the
working in all its effectiveness, of His
Power."
                    Ephesians 3:7 (AMP)

Being a Chaplain is a unique position. Sometimes
people, and staff, think that all we do is encourage offenders,
pat them on the head, and tell them Jesus loves them. Oh, if
only that were true! I asked God for guidelines for being a
Chaplain before accepting the position. We all know that the
whole Bible is one big guideline, but I wanted something

specific, something that would help me to really help the women who were incarcerated at Eddie Warrior. The Lord ministered the following scripture to me early on:

"Mercy and truth are met together"
Psalms 85:10 (KJV)

Mercy and truth are the only *real* answers for all of us. I use this scripture when I talk to inmates and people outside prison ministry. The Mercy of God allows God's hand to reach down to *anyone*, no matter where they have been or what they have done. Praise God for that. But, if I don't tell you the *truth*, your life will never change. There is a holy balance in this scripture.

Chaplaincy is one of the most demanding and yet rewarding ministries you can possibly imagine. It is a ministry that will carry mega Grace and requires mega hard work.

His Place, His Grace—His Will, His Bill.

• Manage anywhere from 300 to 600 volunteers who come into their facility to teach classes and facilitate programs that will help offenders make something of their lives. By manage, I mean keep Program Leaders informed of changes and guidelines, "Do's and Don'ts" and changes in policy for volunteers. Every Group has a Program Leader. Quarterly, I sent out a letter notifying Program Leaders to remind them of existing guidelines. Volunteer Chaplain Mary Painter called them, "Do Better Letters." That worked for me!

Fifty-three religious groups come in to EWCC to minister in church services to the female inmates here. Female offender-pertinent classes are taught. I see once they are on the outside, after they have left prison, they always bring up how when they were first released and trying to find a church home, they really missed Eddie Warrior Correctional Center Church. We had some powerful services. I tell them, repeatedly, before they leave, that churches on the outside will NOT be like here at EWCC. They tease and ask if they can come back to EWCC for the church services!

One thing I always emphasize is that they must find a church and get connected when they get out: No church is perfect, but they must have a home church—that is a part of "protecting what God has done in you here at EWCC." A church keeps you involved, fed, and accountable.

23

> **"Not forsaking or neglecting to assemble together as believers, as the habit of some people, but admonishing, warning, urging and encouraging one another..."**
> **Hebrews 10:25 (AMP)**

• Schedule a monthly calendar that looks like it has more programs than times and ensure all religions are represented in the chapel program. The word chaplain means "servant to all." And we are. We try to locate volunteers for Wiccan, Muslim, and any other religions, as there is a need. Interfaith Council meets bi-monthly with Leo Brown, chaplains and anyone who represents *any* religion, to ensure that the basic religious needs of inmates are met.

A Muslim inmate came to my office frequently to ask me to pray for her family, and to threaten to file a lawsuit against me because I could not locate a Muslim volunteer to come hold Islamic classes. I had tried. I even sent letters to the Masjid in Tulsa to see if we couldn't get a Muslim woman in here to go through the volunteer process and minister to those inmates. I had made contact with a very nice Muslim lady who said she would try to help me out when I needed someone for something specific, but she was too busy to come visit regularly.

When this inmate asked me to pray for her family, I asked her if she would like me to try to get this one Muslim volunteer to come in and pray with her because I only had my way of praying. Every time she would say, "No chaplain, could you just pray for my family?". So I did my best, because I sincerely wanted to help her. About two years later, I ran into her outside of prison. She came up to me and hugged me and said she was no longer Muslim but was now a Christian. I asked her how that happened. She said, "Chaplain, as much as I wanted to file a lawsuit against you, which I thought was part of my duty as a Muslim, whenever you prayed for my family, I could NOT deny that *every* time you prayed for me or my family, I felt the Presence of God. I didn't know what to call it then—but I do now. Thank you, Chaplain.'

• Counsel continuously: through conversation and by example; keeping in touch with Mental Health professionals at the facility and Correctional Officers when inmates are struggling, while holding inmates accountable for their actions and decisions. Inmates are expected to show respect to authorities and to follow the rules. Something we all must do.

• Notify inmates if their family calls to say that their family members are in serious condition in ICU or if they have died. I would say that I would do about four of these notifications per week. First, I verify by calling the hospital, hospice, nursing home or funeral home confirming before I tell an inmate about a serious crisis in their family. There have been times when an ex-boyfriend who abused an inmate on the outside, then tries to harass her on the inside by calling with bogus notifications. I only page the inmate after I have verified the news, then tell her quickly what has happened and give her a free phone call, or more than one, if that family member is critical.

When I did a death notification, I would break the bad news quietly but quickly. I always have a pot of coffee on and when the inmate was trying to absorb the bad news, I would close my office door and offer her a cup of coffee just to give her a minute and some comfort time. I encouraged her to stay in my office for a few minutes before they would face all the inquisitive inmates back in the dorms. Then I say very little and let them quietly have their cup of coffee. And I wait until they say they are ready to go back to the dorm.

This became an outreach to inmates who never came to the Chapel; but they did for this. They have to come to my office when I page them, when I had to give them the bad news. Many said they experienced great peace in our Chapel Building.

Reactions to these emergency notifications vary. Sometimes they almost faint or get very hysterical. Sometimes they just sit down in shock. Other times, they will begin to tell me about this person who died. Frequently, the family member who died is also the one who molested them when they were little. Mixed feelings. Mixed messages. It's a lot to sort out.

Inmates' families frequently have health problems also, so Chaplains handle these emergencies/crises all the time. We send copies of the "Emergency/Crisis" form to Mental Health, Case Managers and Chief of Security, so staff can know what is going on with this particular inmate and be ready to help her. Since most inmates are emotionally

27

fragile (though they might not show it), we keep an eye on them for a few days after a Crisis Notification.

I have found that when I have to tell an inmate their mother has died, and, if mother was on drugs or, even most entirely out of the picture, they are not only mourning their death, but are grieving for what could have or should have been—but *never* was.

Currently, inmates can be transported/accompanied by an officer to view the body of their immediate families privately. No family can be present. Her family must pay for the transport. I don't like this because if the inmate's family has the money, she can go—but if her family does not have the money, she can't.

• Speak outside of their respective facilities at churches or other groups about prison ministry. This enlightens people on the outside who don't know what really goes on in a prison.

• Supervise inmates who work for them in the chapel. We try to mirror the real world by ensuring that every inmate has a job of some sort, and that inmate is held accountable for getting to work on time and *working* while they are at work. We work on developing their character as they grow spiritually and mentally. They will *have* to work when they get out.

One inmate told me one time that when she first got to prison at Eddie Warrior, she thought "cruel and unusual punishment" was having to wake up early, take a shower and come to work all day. I told her that was what the rest of the world, including me, has to do this practically every day of our lives. She said she came from a family who never worked at all. They stole or sold drugs.

I asked her later how she felt about this "cruel and unusual punishment" now that she did the work thing regularly. She hesitated, then replied: "Chaplain, it feels really good – I feel like a real person."

• Pray for many offenders personally or, well, to put it accurately: You just can't trust Christians or Chaplains; they will pray for you behind your back! I have prayed many prayers for the inmates and staff at Eddie Warrior Correctional Center, mainly *declaring* that:

29

Jesus is Lord over Eddie Warrior Correctional Center and the Holy Spirit is working *all* the time!

• Maintain their availability for any staff that need any kind of help—or simply to talk. Staff don't usually like to be seen talking to the Chaplain for any real length of time. They think inmates may think they are weak or have a lot of problems. They must maintain their authority with inmates; they don't want inmates to think they are not in control.

• Attend weekly or bi-weekly Staff meetings, quarterly Chaplain's training and any other trainings expected of them. They meet deadlines for reports set by Wardens, Deputy Wardens, and Leo Brown's office as Head Chaplain. And, like all Department of Corrections employees, they are never, never, never caught up on their work. We never get caught up; we just go home.

• Answer "Requests to Staff" from inmates about different issues: classes; religious dietary changes; etc. There are special diets the Oklahoma Department of Corrections serves inmates if their designated religion requires a special diet. There are probably two or three inmates who profess to really be and are Muslim and they can get a special diet. There are probably 30 who will call themselves Muslim just to get the change in diet. We have to honor whatever they designate as their religion.

• Constantly familiarize themselves with the extensive amount of "OP's" or DOC Guidelines to prevent any type of potential lawsuit, since the majority of inmate lawsuits come through Medical or Religious Rights issues.

• Walk that fine line of being professional, and yet remaining sensitive to the needs of the inmates with whom they work.

Many classes are scheduled and managed and/or taught by the Chaplains. At Eddie Warrior Correctional Center some of the classes taught are: Sexual Abuse Recovery; Abortion Recovery; Codependency; (I call this one "How to Be Jerk Free"); Marriage and Relationships; Parenting From Prison; Breaking Free; Celebrate Recovery; AA/NA; New Life Behavior; Women in Transition (Reentry class); Genesis One (Reentry); Boundaries; Kairos; Victory Bible College; Substance Abuse Education, in addition to the 53 church group services.

I occasionally thought about "goals" that I heard so many preachers talk about: One Year Goal; Two-Year Goal; Three-Year Goal; etc. But I had one overall goal: I wanted to finish a day as a Chaplain without screaming.

During a particularly trying day, God began to lay out a "plan" for the ministry at EWCC. He told me to:

1. Get women saved.
2. Renew their minds.
3. Help their children (who are considered "at risk" children—at risk to end up in prison themselves).
4. Help them reenter society.

Wow, Lord, how do I do all that? He assured me not to be overwhelmed, but to keep these purposes in my heart and HE would bring it to pass. And HE did. God did it and I have simply run to catch up with Him.

• Delight in teasing each other. For example, at one of our trainings each Chaplain was assigned a particular religion to research so we could all be well informed about the basic beliefs of them all. I did not attend. So, when I came to the next meeting, they told me they had just assigned me to get basic principles on "satanism."

The Heart of a Chaplain

For a long time, I was the *only* female chaplain in the state of Oklahoma. The chaplains received me, showing me respect and guiding me in such a kind way. I will always appreciate and respect my fellow chaplains. They are men and women of integrity and strong faith in God. They are dedicated to their ministry as chaplains. They work so hard and really want to make a difference in the lives of inmates.

After I had been working as a Chaplain for about six months, one day I drove home, threw myself on my bed in tears and told the Lord I thought I shouldn't be a Chaplain. The problem: I had to actively recruit volunteers for religions that didn't recognize Jesus as Lord. I cried and, amid my weeping, I told God that I would never do anything that would take away from Jesus, His Name, or His Diety. There was a pause. I think God was waiting for me to get through with my tears.

I was looking for answers, but what I felt I got from the Lord was a question: "Would you rather have someone from a non-Christian faith in your position—your position of influence as a chaplain? I had to think about that. The answer was, of course, "no." When I shared this with a few chaplains, they each assured me that they had been through the same thing. They were such men of God!

> **"Jesus said to him: I am the Way and**
> **the Truth and the Life; no one comes to**
> **the Father except through Me,"**
> **John 14:6 (AMP)**

I realized Jesus can take care of Himself. I set all religious tracts out for inmates to take, and the Christian stuff disappears quickly. The non-Christian stuff is still there. When you are really desperate, your Spirit longs for and will gravitate toward *truth*.

Chaplains are required to have a master's degree, and yet, we make just a little more than a corrections officer. I'm not complaining—it's just a fact. Since chaplains don't really make enough to support themselves on a chaplain's salary, they are usually what is called a bi-vocational pastor. Translation: neither one of their bi-vocational jobs pay them enough money to make a living. Some chaplains pastor churches in *addition* to being a chaplain. Some have wives that work, so they can make it on a chaplain's salary.

Due to increasing medical premiums and no Cost of Living or any other kind of raise for several years—the last three years, I took home $450 less, per month, than I did when I first started working for DOC years ago. This was true of other chaplains. They stayed because they *believed* in what they were doing.

Really, I *loved* being a chaplain and I would have done it for *free*—but I didn't tell DOC that.

Even at that, the chaplains are generous when another chaplain has a need. At one point, I had to take my husband to MD Anderson in Houston for cancer treatment. I was gone almost six months. The Oklahoma Department of Corrections allows employees to donate "hours" (like comp time, sick leave, vacation leave, etc.) to another employee in need. I know that Leo Brown, Head Chaplain, Jim Remer, and several other chaplains AND my Warden and some staff donated so much time to me that *I never missed a paycheck* during that long family leave time. What a blessing they have been to me.

35

So, all the services, programs, all the classes, all the counseling—how does a Chaplain do all that by themselves? They don't...VOLUNTEERS DO!

CHAPTER 5

The Volunteers

"For God is not unrighteous to forget or overlook your labor and the love which you have shown for His name's sake in ministering to the needs of the saints, His own consecrated people,as you still do."
Hebrews 6:10 (AMP)

Prisons would be awful places without the Volunteers who come in faithfully and tirelessly to minister to and help the people behind bars. They do things chaplains cannot do. They are the right arm of the chaplains and the champions of the inmates. They don't get paid, but they are a priceless attribute to the facilities they visit. They hold Church services, teach classes, help offenders find places to live when they get out and counsel and pray with inmates continuously.

Volunteers are an immeasurable influence. They plant incorruptible seed and display excellence, faithfulness, and consistency that most inmates have never seen.

All the groups are anointed and a blessing to the ladies incarcerated at EWCC. For example, the Fort Gibson Church of Christ had been coming in longer than I had been a chaplain. They teach classes every Friday morning, water baptize about 10 women every month and their obvious faithfulness speaks volumes to incarcerated women who have never seen anything close to that kind of dedication.

Since chaplains do not have secretaries or staff—they *really* need help. Since I don't have a secretary, on Secretary's Day I take myself out to lunch. I want to be sure to let myself know how much I appreciate me. Fortunately, different volunteers serve as "Volunteer Assistant Chaplains" in the chaplain's office on a different day each week.

Volunteers fill a consistent need. Volunteers are the greatest resource any Department of Corrections Chaplain has.

There are about 4,000 volunteers statewide going into different prisons in Oklahoma. About 500 volunteers come into minister to the 800-900 females incarcerated at Eddie Warrior.

Volunteers have to go through a full day's training every two years in order to be "badged" by DOC. Poor volunteers. They have to listen to me, or another Chaplain trainer, explain all kinds of procedures, guidelines and concepts to learn about or be refreshed in. The Department of Corrections tells volunteers such things as:

You can declare anything you believe, but you cannot "down" or make derogatory remarks about another religion or group. It's sad that this even needs to be addressed. We should respect each other because every group wants to come in to help inmates change their lives.

> **"And there are distinctive varieties of service and ministration, but it is the same Lord Who is served. And there are distinctive varieties of operation, of working to accomplish things,**
> **but it is the same God who inspires and energizes them all in all."**
> **I Corinthians 12:5 (AMP)**

Sent to Prison

The Oklahoma Department of Corrections requires that all denominations coming into a facility respect each other. We should be able to show respect for one other.

My Dad and I used to tease each other about our different denominations. He asked me why I didn't visit his church more often. I said, "Dad, its' just too quiet for me." I asked him why he didn't come to visit my church more often. He put both hands up in the air (like we do at my church) and said, "Well, sis, when I went to your church, I thought we were being robbed."

Volunteers must be an example of respect to Security personnel.

Volunteers cannot get personally involved with an inmate or their families

Volunteers must dress modestly! I think it is really sad that the Department of Corrections has to tell church people, who make up the majority of DOC volunteers, how to dress modestly: no low-cut blouses, no sleeveless blouses, no tight pants. That means no skintight jeans or pants of any kind.

At Eddie Warrior, I did not allow volunteers to wear jeans. I felt that a level of excellence should be exhibited. To me, it was a privilege to minister to the people incarcerated, so I required that volunteers dress well.

We share about the fact that male inmates may have violence going on frequently, but that female inmates are more manipulative. Manipulation. I didn't know that was a bad word until I came to work in a prison. I thought "manipulation" was God's gift to wives! Who knew? My husband used to tell me the weapons of my warfare were carnal.

It's challenging to hold worship services at Correctional Facilities. You are basically in charge of your service, and you have to do some crowd control when you minister. Volunteers at EWCC have to contend with a lot of nonsense from inmates during service. Most of the women coming out of their dorms for church services are glad to be there and appreciate the volunteers coming to minister to them.

However, there is so much homosexuality among inmates that it becomes a problem during services. Inmates cannot just go into another inmate's dorm and visit with them. They may see them on the yard, but many times they attend church services as "date night." They may play "touchy-touchy" in a not so nice way as they sit on the back row during services.

It is awkward, but necessary that volunteers address this kind of behavior. The volunteer group should have at least one volunteer in the back of the auditorium watching for this. They are instructed to quietly go up to the inmates exhibiting this behavior and correct them—nicely, but firmly. And tell them to put a chair between each other and that they cannot touch. It's a facility rule that inmates are not supposed to touch each other *at all*.

Then the volunteer calls me the next day to tell me what happened. I page those inmates to my office and start off by saying: "I know you two are a "couple", but I'm not going to preach to you about it". They quickly say something like – "Oh, no, Chaplain, we are not like that". I tell them "I don't care whether they are homosexual or not. I don't care if its date night between you two. I want you at the services. The volunteers want you at the services. God wants you at the services, but you will be respectful to the volunteers who selflessly come in here. You will behave and not touch each other or talk or laugh but must be respectful of the services for the hour and a half that services last."

Male volunteers are not allowed to come into Eddie Warrior to hold a service or teach a class without a female volunteer coming in with them. This is to protect them against an accusation. But make no mistake: male volunteers coming in are such a witness to the women incarcerated. They are the only men some of the inmates have ever seen who are sincerely trying to help them without wanting something in return. When a man and wife come in as volunteers, they are setting an example that most incarcerated women have never seen.

I once felt led by the Lord to call one of the Program Leaders of one of the church services that came in to EWCC to come help me as a Volunteer Assistant Chaplain. She agreed to come in, and told me later that God had been dealing with her to come in and help me, but she had argued: "Lord, I don't even like Chaplain McCollum. She's so abrupt. I don't *want* to go in and help her." As she was arguing with the Lord, I called her. She couldn't turn me down.

She later shared with me that before she came on board as a Volunteer Chaplain, people would ask her what a chaplain *really* did. She said she cynically told them: "I don't know what they do or what she (meaning me) really does at all." But, once she had been working with me in the chapel for a few months, she said that her tune changed when people asked her what chaplains did. Her voice went up a few decibels and she said: "You just don't have any idea what we do – we do lots of *everything* all day!" She has been a blessing as a volunteer chaplain for years. I'm so thankful for her. We have laughed together many times about this.

The volunteer chaplains I have Monday through Friday are from different denominations, all amazing working with the offenders and all are role models for the women here. These are volunteers, usually older women, who could be doing something else. Each one is a blessing in her own way. They help me in the office and bring in great classes to teach, but the greatest thing they (and all volunteers) bring into a correctional facility is themselves.

One of the inmates told me she was so grateful that we had taught her "how to be a woman." I told her we never had a specific class addressing that. She explained:

"Chaplain, all my life I have been a lesbian and I was always the aggressor. When Jesus so graciously saved me, I turned from this sin because I knew it was wrong. *However*, I didn't really know how to act like and be a woman. *I learned how to be a woman by watching you and the volunteer chaplains and all the volunteers in general – that's how I learned to be a woman.*"

It's not just the message – it's the messenger.

Our auditorium for monthly church services holds about 180 inmates. I knew we had a problem when Central Control announced over the intercom (after announcing that chapel was now open for evening service), "If you inmates don't quit running to the chapel, I will order all of you back to your dorms". It was "first come, first served" at services and we had been turning inmates away after we filled the auditorium.

Attendance at services were amazing and became so full, we had to divide the yard into Unit A and Unit B and only allow half the yard to attend a certain service one month and then the next month, they would be able to attend the church services they had missed. We spread out the services equally, so all could attend. While church people were talking about praying in "revival", we were experiencing it at Eddie Warrior.

Inmates put volunteers up on a pedestal. Inmates think volunteers walk on water in their spare time and don't talk about anything 24/7 except spiritual stuff.

One ex-inmate called me to say she had attended a church after she had gotten out of prison and that, after the service, the women who she knew from volunteering at EWCC, were talking about life insurance and their husbands, etc. She was shocked. She said she never knew that all these godly women volunteers talked about anything but God. She said they were teasing around, asking each other if their husbands would "knock them off" to get the life insurance they had on them. They were laughing.

She asked me if my husband would knock me off for $20,000 life insurance. I told her: "Heck, he has offered to do that several times to me through our 47-year marriage— for free!"

Prison ministers in general don't get much financial and/or spiritual support from their churches. In fact, many times people really don't understand why they come into prison *so consistently and faithfully*. Understandably, churches give to many missionaries who are such an important part of *any* church's ministry, but prisons are also an area of ministry, really a mission field, that affects us as citizens, not only Christians. Volunteers are not naïve, unsuspecting people who think all inmates are so sweet. *You don't have to be naïve to be compassionate.*

"Be ye therefore wise as serpents;
and harmless as doves."
Matthew 10:16 (KJV)

Volunteers simply see inmates as people who need help. And who better to help them than the Lord?

Before God called me to be a chaplain, I had no use whatsoever for "street people" and "lawbreakers." I thought they should all go to prison and stay there. No wonder my husband had a shocked look on his face when I told him I was called to prison ministry. The thing is—they don't stay in prison. Eighty percent of inmates get out! And they move in next door to your children and grandchildren. If not as a

Christian, simply as a citizen, I would want inmates to come out better than when they went in.

Volunteers have lots and lots and lots of rules and regulations they have to follow. They are subject to search at any time. They have to bring everything in a clear container, they cannot carry messages in and out for an inmate. And through all the training, correction and guidelines they must follow when coming into a prison, they *still* keep coming.

They cannot show preference to any inmate—they must treat them all the same. This is a challenge sometimes. We all respond positively when someone brags on us. The inmates tell volunteers how much they appreciate them and their services or classes, and they really mean it. But volunteers have to be careful that they don't only respond to an inmate who may be a good communicator, because there may be some inmate who is *not* a good communicator, who isn't outgoing with compliments, but who needs just as much attention, if not more. We don't play favorites.

Volunteers may travel one to two hours each way to facilitate a service that starts at 7:45 p.m. and ends at 9:15

p.m. *Then* they drive home, and many have to go to work the next day.

Volunteers are faithful, faithful, faithful. "And the faithful shall abound with blessings!" That is my prayer for them. Volunteers are *role models* for men and women who are incarcerated; many of whom have not had good role models.

Volunteers are a direct answer to the prayers of inmates' moms and dads, grandmothers and grandfathers, praying for help for their daughters, or granddaughters.

I once told God that I think he got things backwards. When we are young and raising our kids, we don't know much, but somehow with His Grace, we get through it and get our kids raised. *Then*, when we are older and have some wisdom, nobody cares! Our adult kids won't take our advice. I can't understand why they won't let us run their lives.

I tell my grown daughters to let me know when I am being overbearing. There's only one letter difference between "mother" and "smother" but once a mom always a mom.

Volunteers are usually older and bring their life wisdom with them to help change the lives of inmates. You don't have to be "sister supremely wise". We learn a lot simply living life—and how valuable they are to women who are incarcerated.

> **"But as for you, teach what is fitting and becoming to sound, wholesome doctrine, the character and right living that identify true Christians."**
> **Titus 2:1 (AMP)**

> **"Stimulate and promote the faith of God's chosen ones and To lead them on to accurate discernment and recognition of and acquaintance with the Truth which belongs to and harmonizes with and tends to godliness."**
> **Titus 1:1 (AMP)**

Volunteer Recognition is a Department of Corrections requirement. We recognize volunteers for their work within the department annually. We usually host a banquet and present plaques for "Volunteer of the Year" and "Volunteer Group of the Year." Jim Remer is the Chaplain of Jess Dunn Correctional facility housing over 1,000 male offenders, one half-mile down the road from Eddie Warrior. Jim and I have worked together for the time he has been a chaplain there. You would think I would be his go-to person for answers to chaplain questions, but it has turned out quite the opposite. I go to him for information; especially when it comes to the wonderful, but somewhat complicated, "Volunteer Database."

It's a little complicated for me, but that's not saying much. I turn to Jim for help on the database, because my grandson can't come down here and help me! Jim is faithful to answer my questions—and faithful to remind me of how *old* I am and affectionately calls me a "charismatic nut-job." I would say that Jim should be on some kind of medication, but really—I think it's too late to help him.

We take turns doing "Volunteer Training." This training lasts all day and wonderful Jim is quick to tell the new volunteers if there is anything they want to know about Oklahoma history concerning corrections, to ask *me* since "Chaplain McCollum is so old she was here for the Oklahoma Land Run." I put up with him anyway.

Sent to Prison

We keep volunteers informed and once a year we have an "Annual Volunteer Appreciation Banquet" for the volunteers. These are usually pretty "tame" in most facilities, but at Eddie Warrior and Jess Dunn—we have a blast. Since we have many of the same volunteers going into both facilities, we do ours together.

Ah, yes—the "Annual Volunteer Appreciation Banquets." We try to have fun. We have different themes. One of our first ones together was a "Western" theme. Jim dressed as a cowboy with a three sizes too small hat, play guns that a two-year-old would carry and chaps. We looked ridiculous. I dressed like a country Dolly Parton. Jim said (in front of everyone): "You don't *look* like Dolly Parton." I said "Yes, I do. I'm built just like her—only upside down."

One year we did a Luau. Jim and I dressed ready for the beach complete with scuba snorkels and masks, rubber duckie inner tubes around our waists, children's arm floaties and large scuba flippers on our feet. We looked ridiculous. The then Director of the Oklahoma Department of Corrections attended this banquet. We got into trouble for inviting the Director without going through our Warden first.

It happened on a "dare." Jim dared me to e-mail the Director of DOC and ask him to attend. I took the dare, totally expecting a "no," if we received any reply at all. Surprisingly, he e-mailed me back saying, "I would love to come, and I will be in the area on that night." We both about fell over. While we were still dressed in our beach attire, the Director got up to speak, and said, "These Chaplains are both fired." He was so gracious to us and joined in on the fun. The next day we were both told to report to the Warden. He wasn't happy we invited the Director without letting him know first. It was like being sent to the principal's office.

One year we did a "Star Trek/Star Wars" theme. I had a "Princess Leia" costume, complete with a "hair bun" on each side of my head, a white robe and, of course, my laser sword. Jim dressed as "Dr. Spock" complete with pointed ears. We looked ridiculous.

We did a Volunteer Banquet that was a "'50s Banquet". We played '50s music. My wonderful husband agreed to dress up as Elvis after three months of nagging him, and it was a "hoot." I know how to nag: I've been married to my Bobby for 47 years. He had an Elvis costume complete with wig and made his grand entrance as an old

Elvis with a cane, who came suddenly alive when we started playing—yes, you guessed it: "Jail House Rock." Was that an appropriate song for a Volunteer Banquet or what? The whole place "rocked"! Our Warden and several staff got onstage and had a hula-hoop contest.

I tease Jim a lot, but really, he has been a good and valuable friend to me over the years. When I was in Houston with my husband at MD Anderson, he called all the time to see how we were doing. Jim is a blessing, a good Chaplain and a fun person to be around.

I LOVE ALL THE VOLUNTEERS WHO COME IN TO EDDIE WARRIOR.

But, before I finish about volunteers, I *have* to tell you about Volunteer Mary Painter.

About 18 years ago, a beautiful young lady came to my office, sat down and, somewhat nervously, introduced herself as the person who was coming in with another volunteer who was teaching "Sexual Abuse Recovery." In a subdued voice, she stated that she wanted to know if she could teach a class independently, rather than alongside the woman who had trained her. Immediately, the Holy Spirit said that I was to "stretch her in her gifts." But, let me make it very clear: Over the years, I tried to obey the Lord, and as I stretched Mary—she stretched me *more*. She taught me grace under pressure, compassion at a deeper level, teaching more effectively and a faithfulness to God that I had never seen displayed by anyone else.

Mary is gifted. She has the "Gift of Giving." She has consistently given of her time, her efforts and her finances to the Chapel work here at EWCC. She has the Gift of Hospitality, the anointing to teach and guide. She has a Pastoral anointing. She is quick to give powerful, forthright counsel to anyone who asks.

> **"He whose gift is practical service, let him give himself to serving; he who teaches, to his teaching; He who exhorts, encourages to his exhortation; he who contributes, let him do it in simplicity and liberality; he who gives and superintends, with zeal and singleness of mind, he who does acts of mercy, with genuine cheerfulness and joyful eagerness."**
> **Romans 12:7, 8 (AMP)**

That's Mary Painter. Mary has been the energy factor behind anything that has been done at Eddie Warrior Chapel Program the last 18 years. She has provided an example of a Christian woman, a teacher who is able to engage even the most hardened of women because of the love and instruction she gives teaching the "Sexual Abuse Recovery", "Abortion Recovery" and "Breaking Free" classes. When she walks into a room, people around her want to be better people. When she teaches a class, she makes the women inmates want to be better women. She always makes every woman feel special, no matter what lifestyle they have led; Mary makes them feel special *not* only to God but to *her*.

She has also been a great source of financial help to the Chapel Program over the years not only out of her pocket, but she is constantly on the lookout for people and organizations who can help and, as a result, has contributed so much to us. She helped by giving hours, days and months to help build the CHAPEL! All of this while she taught Bible studies at her church, and she is—can you believe it?? A jet pilot! Yes, Mary, one of the most beautiful, feminine, humble women I know flies a jet!

Mary keeps all our donated computers running, she buys and generates donations for any classes for anyone. Her church, Bethany Church, is a church that has the "gift of giving." The church has given so much to us—not only money, but they are a "presence" at EWCC. Once a year they bring in 1,000 hot dogs and hamburgers and we set tables out on the Oval (an outdoor area) and Bethany members serve the 800-900 inmates at EWCC.

Mary is the Program leader for Bethany Church. She manages EWCC's "Card Shop" to keep it open. She teaches, counsels, prays and encourages inmates supernaturally. She oversees an offsite account for Chaplains so they can raise money to replace chairs, religious materials, etc. But the most important thing Mary does—she takes me out and buys my lunch every Wednesday, which is the day she serves as a volunteer Chaplain in my office. Once, when she had flown to Europe, I e-mailed her and wrote that she had forgotten to leave me my lunch money. I really want to pay her back some day, but I owe her about half a million dollars for lunch.

Mary is respected by every staff member, Warden, Deputy Warden and Chief of Security that we have had. She obeys *every* rule. If I tried to bring something into the facility that was not allowed, I would get into trouble. Mary could walk in with an elephant on a leash and all they would say to her is "Good morning, Ms. Painter." She respects every officer. She clearly understands Security and that she is ministering inside a Prison. I should be jealous but all I have is admiration, really.

Mary is a gift from God to me. Mary Painter is a woman I deeply respect and she was tirelessly faithful as the impetus behind one of the greatest assets to our Chapel Program—the Chapel itself.

CHAPTER 6

The Chapel

"Take heed now, for the Lord has chosen you to build a house for the sanctuary. Be strong and do it!
        I Chronicles 28:10 (AMP)

"...Fear not, be not dismayed, for the Lord God, my God, is with you. He will not fail or forsake you until you have finished all the work for the service of the house of the Lord."
        I Chronicles 28:20 (AMP)

O Lord our God, all this store that we have prepared to build You a house for Your Holy Name and the token of your presence comes from Your hand and is all Your own."
        I Chronicles 29:16 (AMP)

"...And now I have seen with joy Your people who are present offer voluntarily *and* freely to You.
        I Chronicles 29:17 (AMP)

These are the scriptures God gave me that I stood on as the Chapel was being built. And my personal confession was: "I love rich people and rich people love me." Well, it couldn't hurt!

Leo Brown was the first person to have the God-idea to build a chapel at Eddie Warrior Correctional Center. Leo was still chaplain at Jess Dunn when he called me to discuss the possibility of building a chapel at EWCC. I said, "Can we do that?" I had no idea how we would be able to make this happen. Leo was the first person to think about the possibility of the chapel—but I got the credit for it. I kind of like that arrangement, I have to be honest about that.

Leo was instrumental in establishing an off-site account that every chaplain could use. For instance, a chaplain may need new chairs for his Chapel and let's say someone gives him a check for $300 toward the $1,500 he needs for all new chairs. He has to house the monies somewhere until the amount required has been accumulated; and thus, the offsite account "Oklahoma Corrections Chapel Fund" was set up.

I started sending out letters to volunteers at EWCC and ministries, churches, etc. to raise money for a Chapel. I could not really comprehend the reality of a *real* chapel building. Through the generosity of many people, God helped me raise $40,000 to put in our off-site account. There wasn't any one person who gave a large sum of money, rather it was volunteers giving $10, $20, $30 and some $100. Pastor Billy Joe Daugherty, Pastor of Victory Christian Center in Tulsa at that time, had not seen me in 20 years but he remembered my name when he saw me at prison. He asked me what I was doing, and I told him about the chapel. Pastor Billy Joe was one of the first people to contribute to the chapel.

Then, everything seemed to stall. Even as I made inquiries about metal buildings, and continued telling people about the chapel, I felt stuck. After two years of waiting for something to break, I went to the Lord and told Him I appreciated the $40,000, but that it had been almost two years since I had raised that money. I told Him that if something didn't happen soon, the only honorable thing I could do would be to give each contributor their money back.

Not long after that conversation, a builder shared with Justin Jones, our then Director of Corrections that he had had a vision to build chapels in *every* prison in the State of Oklahoma. WHAT A VISION!!

From this point on, it *was* my vision. I jumped in with both feet. I knew it was my job to do all I could to be a part of this great undertaking.

At first, no one knew which facility would be chosen to be the first of many chapels to be built in Oklahoma. EWCC was chosen because we had raised $40,000 *and* we already had at least 300 inmates on every waiting list for every class. We had the volunteers who were dedicated to this vision.

At the beginning, a meeting was held and a few construction guys, the builder, some Department of Corrections construction people and I gathered around a conference table.

I have to be honest, at first even though it was not going to cost the Department of Corrections any money, the Department representatives were pretty negative. They wanted to make sure the building was built professionally and soundly.

One guy in overalls listened to the negativity and then said, "I can see where you are coming from, but I am the guy who is going to get the ground ready for cement *and* I really think I can do this, since I have been a civil engineer for the last 30 years."

Another guy on the builder's team said, "I think I can manage to ensure that the Chapel will be professionally done and soundly built. My firm constructed the dome on the State Capitol Building."

It never ceases to amaze me the level of excellence that dedicated people have who are so busy, yet who stop everything to do something like build a chapel for inmates they don't even know, at the cost of their time and their expense.

> **"And see, you have the divisions of the priests and Levites for all the Service of God's house, and with you in all kinds of work will be every willing, skillful man for any kind of service."**
> **I Chronicles 28:21 (AMP)**

Please understand, I have considered it a privilege to work for the Oklahoma Department of Corrections. No, they are not perfect. They have a *big* job with a large number of people (staff and inmates) to manage and try to make better and they are consistently underfinanced. The Department of Corrections is filled with dedicated staff, from the newest officer to the directors of the Department.

The head builder for all the chapels built was also a strong fundraiser. He was the type of fundraiser that was aggressive enough to make even the kindest of Christians mad. Angry or not—they wrote checks anyway. It should be noted that all the groups who came in to assist EWCC through the chapel programs and services were kept informed of the progress and subsequent needs to complete the chapel, but it was Christians who contributed to the building project.

During the years that the builder oversaw the building of chapels in various correctional facilities, he was talking to his 10-year-old grandson who was showing him his report card and had been complaining about his grandpa (the builder) being away so much in order to fulfill this task. The builder (grandpa) explained how this was a work for

God and asked his grandson, "Aren't you proud of your grandpa doing all this?" His grandson said, "Yes, it's a good thing," and looking down at his report card said, "But I really miss being with you, so you are getting a "D" in "grandpa."

At one point, someone wanted me to do a little "commercial" about the chapel and how it was built. When I stated that the Christian community was building the chapel, they suggested that I say that the "faith-based community" (rather than Christians), all contributed to the building of the chapel. I kindly, but firmly stated that I would not say that. I love and appreciate *all* the groups that come into FWCC to minister and to encourage, but the ONLY group that contributed financially to the chapel was Christians. People talk—Christians write checks.

I still get credit for building the chapel, but really, God did it. I simply ran to catch up with Him (as usual). Again and again, through the whole process that took several months, Volunteer Mary worked tirelessly and graciously as always. She managed the Chapel account, arranging for churches to bring in lunch or dinner for the volunteers who lived in their RVs for eight weeks right outside the prison fence. She led the way for the construction of the chapel.

She facilitated fundraisers and was the overseer of the finances flooding into the Eddie Warrior Chapel Fund.

It was amazing. We ended up with a 4,800 square foot building; a church building with a great auditorium, built-in water baptismal, three classrooms, an extensive library with literature from all faiths and offices for the ultimately 10 inmates who would work for me in the chapel. We love our water baptismal. We "slam-dunk" about 20 women for Jesus every month in it! Revival!

Inmates were excited about the chapel, too. They came to me and asked if they could donate to the chapel fund. They were proud they were getting a chapel. Some could only tithe about $2 per month. I told them they should be tithing anyway, so if they want to designate it to the chapel fund, it would be fine. I explained it's not the amount of money. God honors the hearts of those who give.

Not long after that, I got a call from the Department of Corrections business office. She asked if I could please tell the inmates *not* to request such small amounts to be taken out of their personal accounts. I told them I was sorry, but I was the one who encouraged them and that it was a good thing. She said we have to go to all the trouble to generate a check for sometimes as small an amount as $1. I didn't say anything else—and neither did she.

I tried not to get frustrated with *any* department within the Oklahoma Department of Corrections. *All* staff, at any level work, so hard for so little pay and, whether they realize it or not, by working hard they enable staff, Chaplains and volunteers to make a difference in the lives of men and women who are incarcerated.

After the cement was poured for the foundation, inmates who were working for me asked if they could write scriptures in the cement before it was covered with carpet. They wrote scriptures all over the 4,800 square feet of cement—talk about standing on the Word!

Remember when I said that the color of everything in the prison was gray? Well, when it came to put down the carpet in the chapel, I asked the warden if I could carpet the chapel with another color other than gray. The warden stated that he was so tired of the whole chapel thing that I could use any color I wanted! We chose a shade of burgundy-purple. It was colorful and so were the 180 chairs in the chapel.

Mary and I didn't agree on all the color and, we argued about it, but at least it wasn't gray!!

Mary had bought some paint for our smallest classrooms. It was a beautiful pink—pale pink we thought. But it was completed while we were out to lunch and when we came back, it was *really* pink! But all of us *loved* it. It became a special room where we held the smaller classes such as, Abuse Recovery and Abortion Recovery. It's now referred to as "The Pink Room." It really is conducive to make inmates feel "safe" as they take these important classes. Also—it's pretty—and we *like* pretty.

As a matter of fact, an ex-inmate who had changed his life and was now a Pastor at a church in Tulsa had his church pay for the carpet and tile in the new chapel. What a blessing!

Also, I had asked if the area just 25 feet from Central Control could be the spot to build the chapel. It was close for security purposes and great for volunteers who previously had to walk all the way to the back of the prison property for their services or classes.

Not long after the chapel was completed, I thanked the Warden at that time for letting me have that particular portion of the property to build the chapel on. Employees and security were surprised the warden agreed to let me have that area. He stated, "Chaplain, I have been a Warden in several facilities, and every chaplain who worked for me always said they were going to build a Chapel—and none did. If I thought for one minute you were *really* going to build a Chapel, I would never have agreed that you could have that space." Well, God is GOOD.

I must brag on my husband again. All the places we traveled to raise funds, all the time spent doing so many things involved with building the chapel was time-consuming and my husband was consistently supportive. When I felt like it wasn't going to be where and how we needed the building to be, my husband supported and encouraged me. He was *always* my cheerleader.

New Building, New Life in the Spirit

I have to explain the wonderful way God the Father, God the Son, and God the Holy Spirit worked in our powerful, anointed Water Baptisms.

Before we were in the new chapel building; back when we were in the basement of the Gym, we had a portable baptismal—with only cold water. And I do mean ice-cold water. And still, inmates requested to be water baptized, in spite of very cold temperatures.

A volunteer helped me with the actual dunking of people, and a startling thing happened. The Holy Spirit began to give most (not all) of the inmates a "word from the Lord" through me as they came up out of the water. God did this in such a powerful way, that the inmates had tears streaming down their cheeks.

I was pretty shocked myself that God had used me in such a way. But, when I came back to work after a weekend, three inmates were standing outside my office waiting for me and were crying. They said that God gave a "word" to the other inmates who participated in the water baptism, but they didn't get one. They said God must not love them as much as the inmates who got a "word" from Him, and they had cried all weekend.

I tried many times to explain how the gifts of the Spirit operate, but I could not convince them that God loved them just as much as the other inmates who were baptized. They left sad. This happened again at the next three baptisms we did. The inmates who did not get a specific word from the Lord were devastated. My explanation didn't seem be understood.

I know many people believe in the gifts of the Holy Spirit as mentioned in I Corinthians 12, but they don't believe that you can believe for a Word for everyone you may be ministering to, because the gifts are operated "as the Spirit wills."

I told the Lord that I didn't know what else to do. I either needed a "word" by the Spirit for every woman getting baptized or I needed to not have any. It was amazing what a stir this caused on the yard, at least for those who participated in chapel stuff. They valued a "word from the Lord."

After much prayer, I sensed the Lord said he would give me a word from Him by the Holy Spirit for each inmate who was baptized. He said that some would contain the "word of wisdom" or the "word of knowledge" or any of the gifts listed in I Corinthians 12; some would simply be words of edification, exhortation and comfort—but that each one would get a genuine word from the Lord, in accordance with what the Spirit wills.

> **"Now about the Spiritual Gifts brethren, I would not have you ignorant."**
> **I Corinthians 12:1 (KJV)**

> **"Now there are diversities of gifts, but the same Spirit. And there are differences of administrations, but the same Lord and there are diversities of operations, but it is the same God which worketh all in all."**
> **I Corinthians 12:4-6 (KJV)**

Debra and Larry Kerns helped me with water baptisms for years. They were sensitive to the Holy Spirit and faithful to pray for the baptism services.

When we got into the new chapel building, the gifts of the Holy Spirit did not diminish, but increased in anointing. But this presented another problem. The words came through me, but I did not know ahead of time what the Holy Spirit would say and, I certainly could not remember each word given to 20 or so inmates. It meant so much to the ladies getting baptized, but they could not remember it all either.

But the inmate clerks knew what to do. They said, "Chaplain, let us record the words as you give them. Then [we will] transcribe those words into a bookmark and laminate the bookmark and give it to each inmate who had received a word." Honestly, some women who worked in the chapel said inmates who had been released four or five years earlier or so, still had their bookmark they kept in their Bibles. It meant that much to them.

This is how it happened. As an inmate descended the stairs into the baptismal waters, the Holy Spirit gave me one distinct word. Then, when they come up out of the water, I would hold their hand and the Holy Spirit would give me the rest of the word.

I had an inmate who came to watch the baptism tell me that she had just come to see how phony all that "Word stuff" was, because she knew several of the girls getting baptized that I knew nothing about at all. They hardly ever came to the chapel. So she knew the "words" given them would probably not fit them. But after the water baptisms she said, "Chaplain, every word you gave over these women you didn't know was right on for that inmate. You nailed it every time with each woman as they came out of the water." She apologized for setting out to prove me phony. I told her I certainly wasn't going to hold that against her.

> **"Do not quench suppress or subdue the Holy Spirit. Do not spurn the gifts and utterances of the prophets. Do not depreciate prophetic revelations nor despise inspired instruction or exhortation or warning."**
> **I Thessalonians 5:19, 20**
> **(AMP)**

I'm totally convinced that the Holy Spirit moved through me because inmate chapel workers would literally get down on their knees in the sanctuary before the baptisms started and pray, pray, pray for the water baptism services.

They would literally get down on my knees in the staff restroom and pray before a baptism service. I wanted to do this, but I needed help getting up! Prior to the actual immersion water baptisms, I ministered the same scriptures every time we had a baptism service:

"We were buried therefore with Him by the baptism into death, so that just as Christ was raised from the dead by the glorious power of the Father, so we too might habitually live and behave in newness of life. For if we have become one with Him by sharing a death like His, we shall also be one with Him in sharing His resurrection by a new life lived for God. We know that our old, unrenewed self was nailed to the cross with Him in order that our body which is the instrument of sin might be made ineffective and inactive for evil, that we might no longer be
the slaves of sin."
Romans 6:4-6 (AMP)

"And baptism, which is a figure of their deliverance, does now also save you from inward questionings and fears, not by the removing of the outward body filth bathing, but by providing you with the answer of a good and clear conscience, inward cleanness and peace before God because you are demonstrating what you believe to be yours through the resurrection of Jesus Christ."
I Peter 3:21 (AMP)

I encourage those who were going to be baptized to ask God for a specific request when they go under the water; some sin or secret unholy attachment to be delivered from when they come up or believe for a healing—or whatever they need from God. Supernatural things happened frequently because of the intense prayer of the chapel inmate clerks.

During one baptism, an inmate came out of the water and the Holy Spirit gave her a Word. But as she started to climb the stairs out of the water, I told the volunteer helping with the service to "dunk her again." The volunteer said, "Chap, all these years, you have never asked me to do that." I told him, "Yes, I know—but dunk her again anyway. He did. She left crying. She came to my office early Monday morning to talk about her getting "double dunked."

She said, "At first, Chap, I got my feelings hurt when you asked to have me go back under the water. I thought maybe there was something wrong with me, but now I know what it was. Even though it has been a long time since I was brutally raped at age nine, I woke up *every* morning feeling "dirty" all these years. But I felt something "come out" of me after that second time. I didn't know what that was, but for the first time since I was nine years old, I woke up and I felt clean. And I have felt clean ever since." I believe that God wanted to free me through that second dunk.

"All these gifts, achievements and abilities are inspired and brought to pass by one and the same Holy Spirit, who apportions to each person individually exactly as He chooses."

I Corinthians 12:11 (AMP)

"Besides this evidence it was also established and plainly endorsed by God, Who showed His approval of it by signs and wonders and various miraculous manifestations of His Power and by imparting the gifts of the Holy Spirit to the believers according to His own will."

Hebrews 2:4 (AMP)

CHAPTER 7

The Staff

Staff who work in prisons are unique people. The job is demanding, and the pay is low, low, low. The atmosphere can be frustrating and, sometimes a little frightening, but they *do* their job. Not only Chaplains, but all employees of the state, never get caught up. I often tell people I work with crazy people—and I don't mean the inmates! I'm teasing. They are committed people doing a hard and thankless job. They handle inmates, who they are trying to help, who hate them. Some staff are really trying to help inmates; others consider it just a job. But they do their very best. I have met some very dedicated, caring staff.

Case Managers manage the time, cases, sentence requirements and reevaluate every inmate every 90 days. They are so busy, and their offices are in the middle of the dorm they manage. They are buried in paperwork. They evaluate the inmate's attitude and find out what classes they attend. Inmates may be on Level 1, 2, 3 or 4. Each level comes with more privileges. Inmates must show they are trying to do the right thing. Level 4 inmates are supposed to be a blessing to the facility and to other inmates and must maintain their level. Basically, we are rewarding good behavior and hard work.

Food Service. Food service feeds 800 women three times a day, seven days a week. Feeding all these inmates is a huge task; especially when they also feel the lack of money, but they feed inmates *every* day. They start around 2:00 a.m. to prepare breakfast. It's easy to criticize what you don't have to do. Darryl Gandy is the Food Service supervisor, and he was my prayer buddy.

Medical. Almost every inmate thinks that our medical department is trying to hurt them. I also realize that medical personnel can be abrupt; they are overworked, also. If an inmate is ill, she requests an appointment by a "Request to Staff" and she will be able to see our nurses and/or doctor who are on call, all the time. If there is something our Medical can't handle, the inmate is taken offsite to a hospital if an emergency or a specialist if necessary.

79

I ask inmates who are unhappy with Medical: "So, when you were out doing drugs, you got your pap smear and breast exam every year—right? No, they didn't, but we do them here at EWCC. I have been frustrated at Medical at times when I felt that an inmate was not being taken seriously, but really, incarcerated women, have abused their bodies for years and have many health issues. And they are experiencing pain that they never felt before because they were high on drugs all the time.

I had one inmate clerk who was slipping in her attitude, was frequently in tears over small things and struggling emotionally. I called her into my office and told her what I observed. I asked her if she was on medication from Medical. She said she was "standing in faith" for being healed emotionally and had quit taking her medication. I told her this decline had gone on for several months and she needed to get back on her medication. The percentage of women incarcerated who are on medication for mental or emotional imbalance is quite high. She said she thought God would be pleased that she was standing in faith. I told her that God was proud of her, but that His Divine Will is that she be *well* and *whole,* and that medication, doctors, and mental health professionals are a blessing from God to that end.   I told her that we have great Mental Health professionals on the compound.

> **"Every good gift and every perfect, free,**
> **large and full gifts are from above; and**
> **come down from the Father**
> **of all that gives light."**
> **James 1:17 (AMP)**

Doctors and medicine are "good and perfect" gifts from God.

Education: Staff at Eddie Warrior are *wonderful.* They test all inmates when they arrive and teach inmates to read, and how to earn their GED. Some inmates advance to take college courses. Educators face the challenge of helping women learn who are very far behind in their education. In order to get their GED, which is considered a full-time job for an inmate, they have to pass the same tests as someone would on the outside, including math, etc. (I probably couldn't pass the math portion myself).

Inmates think of themselves as stupid because they have trouble getting back on the education wagon to pursue their education. Both the teachers and I tell them they are *not* stupid. They just haven't been to school for a long time, and quite frankly, they have done drugs to the extent that it has clouded their minds. *But because God is so good, He restores them mentally and emotionally* in a powerful way. In my experience, it takes *time*.

At GED Graduation, which happens about three times a year, inmates are allowed to wear caps and gowns and receive their diplomas. Graduates "walk the Oval." Inmate dorms all face the Oval. All the inmates clap and cheer for them as they walk from Education to the chapel where graduation is held. Even the hard to handle inmates cheer them on. They value success in other inmates' lives. Some inmates' jobs as tutors help the women incarcerated, but the real "movers" in Education are professional, caring, patient, kind, encouraging *teachers*.

Career Tech: Inmates who are discharging within a certain time frame can apply to attend. The staff at Career Tech teaches inmates how to *get* and *keep* a job. Career Tech instructors are very caring and desire to see incarcerated women succeed when they leave. Still, they teach them a variety of skills and help them get placed in jobs after they discharge.

Not all inmate's education goals are the same, however. Once, several years ago, several inmates accessed the Internet without permission. Normally, they would never have access to the Internet. They launched their own website, "Jail Babes.com" where they advertised their names and DOC numbers and started a following on the Internet getting people to send them money. Of course, before it went very far, our security officers stopped it dead in the water!

In my 22 years as a Chaplain, we have had some wonderful Wardens, Deputy Wardens and Chiefs of Security. I have truly appreciated all of them, but quite frankly, some of these key people were not on the same page, or deliberately stood in the way of some positive programs for the chapel that I felt were needed.

It is unscriptural to wish anyone to lose his job. I have not cursed someone in hopes that they would leave, but I have "blessed them out" at times. What I mean is, I would pray something like this: "Lord, this person is affecting what you want to do here in a negative way. Please bless them with a promotion out of here. Bless them with a promotion, position and more money". I've only done this about four times in my 22 years as a Chaplain. That *does not* mean that all the people who have worked at EWCC who got a promotion was the result of my praying, but some people who needed to go, went! There is a spiritual principle regarding who is in Leadership.

Warden Sharon McCoy was our Warden at EWCC for five years. She was a strong Christian and wasn't afraid to speak up, *but* she did correct you when necessary. Even in the midst of turmoil, Warden McCoy made you feel valued and appreciated. She always acted professionally and was always ready to laugh. A true team builder, she brought that special gift to the table at Eddie Warrior Correctional Center. The inmates had the utmost respect for her. The chapel programs were the strongest when she was a Warden. We were a dynamic duo. It starts at the top. I want to be like her when I grow up.

Correctional Officers at Eddie Warrior are my heroes. They made me feel safe and secure. They are responsible for the whole facility. They have a shift change every quarter; they bring order to the facility so that staff can do their programs. Order is needed to maintain an atmosphere where God can get things done in the chapel.

Even staff sometimes gets frustrated at security rules, but officers have reasons behind every rule. They don't just lay awake at night and think up rules.

Correctional Officers are good people trying to make a living for their families. I have seen younger, potentially great officers who really consider their job opportunity as a way to provide for their family, and an opportunity to help people, but they struggle with the job itself.

> **"For civil authorities are not a terror to people of good conduct, but to those of bad behavior. Would you have no dread of him who is in authority? Then do what is right and you will receive his approval and commendation."**
> **Romans 13:3 (AMP)**

I asked one new, very nice young officer how he liked his job. He dropped his head and said, "I thought I could come here and make a living for my family and, at the same time make a difference in the lives of inmates, but I may have to quit." I asked if it was the low salary? He said, "No, chaplain, it's that we are so short-handed that I have had to work three shifts back-to-back. I don't mind the shift work itself, but I didn't know I wouldn't be home with my family, that I would be away from them so much."

The sad truth is that the pay is so low that we have trouble keeping officers. The ones that stay have to work so many shifts and hours. Officers must walk a "tightrope" too. Some want to make a difference and do a good job, but they have to be so careful not to be too nice or too friendly to inmates. Remember, some are men in a female facility like Eddie Warrior and they must keep up that precarious wall of being somewhat detached. They are in positions of authority over people who, by and large, hate authority. Correctional officers have the greatest responsibility in *any* facility and are sometimes the *least* appreciated. Again, they are my *heroes*.

Chiefs of Security: I always had favor with our Chiefs of Security. They were very kind to me, even when they weren't too sure about what was going on "over there in the chapel."

One time we were able to take an inmate to a deathbed visit for immediate family whose death was imminent. My responsibility was to verify through a hospital or hospice, that the death of the person was imminent. Two officers would escort the inmate to the deathbed visit. Usually after we got the inmate back to the facility after such a visit, we would soon get a call from the inmate's family stating the family member they visited had passed away. One particular time, we had a lot of deathbed visits and subsequent deaths of family members.

However, a group of inmates came to me wanting to form a prayer group to pray for these deathbed visits. The purpose of the group was for the people who were so close to death, would be raised up healed! I assured them it would certainly make a difference, and told them that, with God, all things are possible. I shared a little about intercessory prayer and encouraged them. They began to take their authority and moved with compassion, they prayed, and prayed, and prayed.

So as this rash of deathbed visits was taking place— inmates prayed as each inmate went out—that their loved one would *live* and *not die.*

This went on for months. I was called to the Chief of Security's office, and I sensed his discomfort. He looked at me, then he looked down at his desk. He said, "Chap, I know you are diligent to do whatever Security asks you, but are you sure you are verifying that these people's deaths were imminent? Because, well—*they aren't dying."*

As he was my Chief of Security, I didn't want to show any disrespect. I said "Chief, a group of inmates came to me and wanted to pray and intercede [for] all these people dying; their prayers are working." My professional Chief was dumbfounded at this answer. He just shook his head. I reassured him that I was diligent in my obligation to check for verifications of these incidents. He looked up at me and smiled a weak smile. Then he said, "Okay, Chaplain." I left acknowledging him with a respectful look and sensed a spiritual "giggle" and a "praise God" rising in my heart. I could not help but smile all the way back to the Chapel. Prayer *changes* things.

We had waves of healings. Women prayed—and healings *happened.* My husband came in for a few months to preach and prayed for an inmate who had been diagnosed with breast cancer. Her sister and her mother had both died of breast cancer. She had been to "outside medical" and the diagnosis was verified. When we detect something with an inmate, but need confirmation or further diagnostic tests, etc., we take them outside the compound for further help.

She had been told that she had breast cancer and they planned to do surgery. After being prayed over, she went back to the onsite doctor at the facility, and she could not find the lump. She sent the inmate to outside medical people and they reported that they could not find it either. It was gone.

I spoke to her two years later, after she got out of prison and she was still healed. Sometimes I will see an ex-inmate working a job after they get out of prison, and they will remind me, "Chaplain, do you remember the time you sent me out on a deathbed visit to see my brother? He lived—he did not die." God is so good!!

One incident that included the Chief of Security started one day in my office. I heard my chapel clerk, an inmate who was in my office helping me open some religious mail, scream, "Chaplain!" I asked her what was wrong. She had a very large, white envelope and said, "Oh my gosh, Chaplain – Look what's in here!" The envelope was addressed to an inmate and the return address label was from a well- known ministry. You could tell the ministry's label had been cut out and pasted on the envelope. The inmate's boyfriend on the outside had taken a label of this ministry and put it as the return address, so we would think it was only religious mail and give it to the inmate. *Every piece* of mail, religious or not, is opened when it comes in to EWCC.

Inside this envelope was a small plastic bottle of Vodka, a camera, and some revealing night clothes, to put it delicately. The inmate was going to take pictures of herself and then send them back to her Mr. Yum-Yum.

I immediately called Security and told them to come get the package. When the officer got there, he said so this ministry sent an inmate this stuff? I said, "*No*. The label was put on there by the sender, but the sender was NOT this ministry." He shrugged his shoulders and took the envelope.

Not long after that, the Chief of Security called me and said: "Hey, Chap, I hear you have really "got it going on" over there in the religious area. He then burst out laughing. I know the return label was bogus, but – *Wow, Chap!*". We both laughed for a long time.

Staff, including me, work together with Security as a team. For instance, we have a "Critical Incident Team." A critical incident would be like a riot or a hostage situation or something major that happens at a facility. I am on that team to help coordinate a particular aspect of it. Even though something like this has never happened at EWCC, we do drills to ensure that we know what we are doing in a major situation. When he asked me what I would be doing during a critical situation, I said I was going to be climbing the perimeter fence praying for you all the way home—I'm not staying for the party!

Volunteers have a tendency to think that officers are rude and uncaring. I have two thoughts on that. First of all, security officers aren't friendly to volunteers when they come in. This is because they are NOT maître d's, they are officers.

Second, volunteers think that officers don't seem very impressed with inmates going to church in the Chapel. You see, volunteers and I see inmates at their best. They are at church. However, officers see inmates jump up and down and get all "spiritual" in Chapel, but then go back to their dorms and use the "F" word dozens of times, have relationships with their girlfriends, lie and steal.

Let's Talk a Little Bit About "Jailhouse Religion"

Inmates can truly participate in a church service, but when they go home (or to their dorm), they don't act the same—like Christians on the outside sometimes do.

Many times, inmates go forward and are sincere at the moment, but then you don't see them come back. Many inmates may go forward to the altar/front for prayer or salvation or healing, but then they don't return–like Christians on the outside sometimes do.

Inside prison OR outside the walls: it's more than simply "believing" in Jesus. You could take a survey inside or outside prison and nearly everyone "believes" in Jesus, but the Bible says you must RECEIVE Him." It is RECEIVING HIM INTO YOUR HEART that is the key.

> **"But to as many as did receive and welcome Him,**
> **He gave the authority, power, privilege, and right to become the children of God…"**
> **John 1:12 (AMP)**

I'm reminded of the Parable of the Sower. Sometimes the seed just doesn't seem to "take," but remember: any seed planted about Jesus is "incorruptible seed." It will remain.

Sometimes, officers shared with me something humorous that happened to them as they carried out their duties.

One officer shared that as he was walking around the prison fence, he came upon a woman who was trying to throw something over the fence to an inmate. She kept trying to throw it ("it" being drugs or alcohol or tobacco) over the high prison fence, but she couldn't throw hard enough, so was not successful. The officer said he stood watching her try to throw it over the fence for several minutes. She was oblivious to the officer watching her. The officer finally said, "Ma'am," I don't think you are going to get that over the fence. You need to come with me."

She was the inmate's mother.

Another time an officer told me she found two inmates in the shower together. When she said she was going to write them up for a "sexual" misconduct, the girls said they were showering together to save DOC some water.

Prior to budget cuts several years ago, Eddie Warrior had about 100 inmates to a dorm. Each dorm had a Case Manager, a Counselor, and a unit secretary. After the budget cuts, there is only one Case manager per dorm of 120 inmates and no Counselor or Unit Secretary.

It's not just Eddie Warrior either. A program for rehabilitation of male inmate sex offenders was beginning to show great results, but this program was cut due to a lack of funding.

I think people think any money allocated from State funds to the Department of Corrections is giving money to inmates. It's not. Money allocated to DOC enables us to adequately teach and help change inmate behavior. And it helps us keep good people running our facilities.

Yet due to the lack of adequate salaries, we lose employees constantly. The workload is ridiculous, and the pay is very low. They look for other jobs and they get them. They quit DOC. You really can't blame someone who gets a chance to better himself or herself and their families. Nor can you blame them for wanting a job with less pressure to do the impossible.

CHAPTER 8

Inmate Classes

I went into the prison system to find and minister to "inmates." Instead, I found WOMEN: broken women; desperate women; weary women; emotionally worn women.

Female inmates are individuals. Sometimes when we talk about "inmates" in a general way, we may leave the impression that they are all alike—they are not! However, they do have some basic attitudes, issues and challenges that are common to most inmates.

I always have a small percentage of female inmates who tell me: "Chaplain, I was raised right; this was not my parent's fault. I was disobedient, got in with the wrong crowd, started doing drugs and then drugs started doing me."

But more often, they came from horrible backgrounds. I will cover this in more detail in the female "inmate pertinent" classes they so desperately need and programs that their children need. Renewing the mind is *vital* and it is done in classes we teach. As we cover each class, you will get a more accurate picture of female inmates—where they are coming from and what they are dealing with. This is where the "renewal of the mind" comes in.

Establishing productive habits by example are built into the content of each class. Their lives have been totally unstructured. When you take a class, you have to be on time and you can't miss too many classes. The inmates ask why I'm so strict about this. I explain it's because they will have to have these habits in order to keep a job when they get out. They need practice managing their own lives.

Classes are taught by volunteers. Some volunteers think they are not qualified to teach some of these classes because they have never "been there and/or done that." Secular studies show that having been a victim can give you a special empathy for teaching a class. They also show that someone who has *not* been one, makes for a very healthy instructor, who shows others what "normal" is—whatever "normal" is. I went through this myself.

The Sexual Abuse class needed an instructor. I tried to explain to God that I had never experienced that, so I obviously could not teach it. Have you ever tried to explain something to God? Like He didn't know about it—anyway, bottom line, I had an impression from Him, not an audible voice. 'So, who is doing the healing here? You and your life experience? Or Me and My Word?' I shut up and taught classes.

Minds are renewed. Women are set free emotionally and mentally. Attitudes, perspectives, actions and good decisions are made by inmates, when inmates take *classes.*

> **"And be ye not be conformed to this world, but be ye transformed by the renewing of your mind, that ye may prove what is that good, and acceptable, and perfect will of God.**
> **Romans 12:2 (KJV)**

A side note: Women sign up for a Sexual Abuse Recovery class or any class, but if you put up a signup sheet in a men's facility for Sexual Abuse Recovery class, you will get no takers. To me, this is really sad. I believe almost as many men were abused as little boys, but their masculinity will not allow them to participate.

Men have a more difficult time opening up about negative things. Whereas women will tell you their life story after you have known them for about a week.

Whether a class is faith based or not, I always pray that I will impart truth and wisdom to the women attending the class. Inmates sign up for classes because some of them give her time credit for taking the class. Here again, inmates who really don't want to come to the chapel for services will come for a class so they can get credits. But when they get there, the class changes their way of thinking, and the Holy Spirit gets to work.

Are the classes worth all the effort? YES! An inmate once told me, "Chaplain, if you don't get help at Eddie Warrior, you just don't want it." Education, chapel classes, church services: it's all a win-win deal."

CHAPTER 9

Sexual Abuse Recovery

Sexual Abuse Recovery – A 12 Week (small) Class.
Everyone gets a book.

This class is not professional therapy; it's a 12-week small class with an accompanying book, *Shelter From the Storm*. It's a faith-based Sexual Abuse Bible study, but anyone, any religion or no religion are welcome to attend the class because there are such powerful truths in the curriculum.

The reason this is such an important class for incarcerated women is because approximately 25 percent of women outside of prison report being sexually molested as little girls. Of course, many don't report, even as adults because of shame and guilt.

However, in the female inmate population, approximately 75 to 80 percent have been molested as little girls. I have heard other statistics, but this is in line with what I have seen over the 22 years as a chaplain. We don't make it an "excuse" for their behavior, but it is a root reason for their negative choices. There is a common pattern of behavior and decision-making when sexual abuse occurs.

And please note that a little girl can be sexually abused even though she has never been touched. How? They are made to watch their mom and her boyfriend or made to watch porn or other things. Their innocence has been taken and wrong stimulation takes place. They, too, have been sexually abused.

Here are the common threads that run through incarcerated females who have experienced this degradation. They carry the guilt and shame of the abuse, even though it's not their shame to bear. The molester should be ashamed. They carry shame because their body (flesh) may have responded in a way that they, as little girls, don't understand and cannot identify. They didn't want it, but their physical bodies responded to the abuse.

Guilt, shame and condemnation are reinforced by low self-esteem. I know that is sometimes an overused phrase, but it still applies to inmates as a whole. Most molesters are family or friends of family. When families find this out—most other family members are *not* supportive.

Some inmates have had babies by their mothers' drug dealers, so their moms can get drugs.

Here are some all too frequent and common family reactions to a little girl trying to tell whoever she runs to for comfort or help after she has been molested. It's usually her mother, if she is around.

"I just can't believe you are having sex with my boyfriend." Yes, that happens frequently and yes, the usually the answer is not put as nicely.

"What did you do to make him do this to you?"

"I don't believe you. My boyfriend wouldn't do that."

"Don't tell anyone—you'll get us all in trouble."

Most of the time, because of the negative atmosphere of their home, they just don't tell. They see these things going on all the time even though it's not their fault. They hate authority, because to a child, the adult who abused them is an authority figure.

This lack of support reinforces the self-esteem of the victim because they feel they must have been partially responsible, and they are not worth as much as mom's boyfriend. Many in the class tell me their mom *still* lives with the abuser.

One inmate told me that she ran away from home when she was 11. I asked why and she said she was tired of her mother standing her out on the street corner with a sign hanging from her neck stating: "Will trade for drugs."

One said that her dad didn't really abuse her. She said, "He was just having sex with me to help me get ready to have sex when I got old enough to date."

One inmate said her mother used her to get drugs and that by age 10, she was able to have sex anyway anyone wanted it. But she was quick to tell me, and the class, that she wasn't always abused because she agreed to it after a while. I asked her what she meant by that? She said once she had sex as a 10-year-old with a man about 40 years old, but that it wasn't abuse since she offered herself to him. I asked her why she didn't consider that as abuse? She stated, "Well, chaplain, I just offered myself to him and what's a guy supposed to say when a girl offers him sex?" I said, "Well, how about 'No'?" She said, "But he's a guy." We then had a discussion in the class about how we are taught that men can't say "No" to sex, but they can. The Bible doesn't say, "Thou shalt not commit adultery or fornication– *unless you are a guy*." No, men are not only allowed to say "No," but are expected by God to say "No". This produced a great discussion on responsibility, sexuality and self-esteem.

One girl said her mom went out drinking all the time and would always leave her with her grandma and grandpa. Mom thought she was doing great to make sure her daughter was with her grandparents while she ran around. However, her grandmother would dress her granddaughter up in a sexy nightie to have sex with her grandfather every night she was there.

Results of the abuse cause suppressed feelings of anger, hurt, shame, fear, loneliness, inability to trust, hate for authority figures and prevents healthy intimacy in relationships. Also, abuse victims do not mature as normally as they should and struggle with things that we take for granted.

There is an inmate who had two children by her biological father by the time she was 15. After a few years, she finally freaked out and left her "home" and kids and just went plain crazy. You can imagine how confused and wounded she was. After several years of that, she missed her two kids, who were still living with their father/grandfather. She tried to help her kids, but someone reported her. The father got 20 years for the molestation. She was given 20 years for "failure to protect" (her children). When she was at EWCC, sometimes I would just let her sit in my office most of the day, so she would feel safe. Once during outcount, when every inmate is accounted for, we found her in the back room of the chapel curled up in a corner. She is still serving time. She loves the Lord. She struggles through each day.

One inmate shared that she lived in what would be considered a horrible part of town and her mother was hardly ever around. But when mom came home and groceries were needed, her mother would dress her up to look older—makeup, hair and clothes—and send her a few doors down to ask for milk or whatever and, of course, they "paid" for it with her body. She was 11 years old.

One young inmate said she can never forget that her stepfather had sex with her every night since she was 8 years old. She said she was so confused because the next morning, he would get up and preach as a pastor of a church every Sunday—and everyone loved him. She has had a hard time receiving Jesus and you can understand why. It's easy for us to look back and separate the facts, but as an eight-year-old, she could not figure it all out.

A little girl may hate the act but love the abuser. This causes mixed feelings and confusion. Every little girl wants attention from her father, but she may put up with the abuse because she is so hungry for attention.

The book we use is very powerful and faith based. It was a stretch for the women to work through it because each unit of the book was a challenge. In one unit, we discuss being angry and assigning appropriate responsibility to the perpetrator. It may seem strange, but many times a little girl—especially when the perpetrator is someone they love (father, grandfather, etc.). They will say things like, well, I can't really blame my stepfather: he was lonesome, and Mom was pretty mean to him. They try to excuse the perpetrator because they love him. *Mixed messages*. And when you are little, you can't sort it out. So—in that unit, we gave the inmates taking the class the freedom to be angry towards the perpetrator.

As we went around the classroom to discuss this particular unit of the book, most of the women made excuses and said they weren't really mad. This is sometimes a very difficult class. At the end of the table, one inmate said in a very loud voice, "Well, I hate my dad for doing that to me. I hate him and hope he burns in hell forever for doing it." She definitely had this unit down pat! The other girl's kind of laughed, but it opened up a discussion about hate, forgiveness, and being realistic about assigning appropriate responsibility.

Many inmates have a head knowledge of God and really want to love Him, but they have a hard time knowing Him deep down in their hearts, because they need to be healed there and it affects her faith. She has to grow in trust.

During the last class, the inmates who have completed the book write down the names of anyone they need to forgive on a small sheet of paper. They include themselves. We have a pretty bowl of water in which we put all the lists at one time. We stir it with a pretty cross. The papers with all the names for forgiveness completely disappear as we stir the papers in the water with the cross. I use magic paper that dissolves in water. Sometimes the inmates taking the class will just silently stare at the water for as long as 15 minutes without a word from anyone. It is such a powerful visual: The beautiful cross floats on top of the now clear water.

> **"The Spirit of the Lord is upon me because He hath anointed me to preach the gospel to the poor. He has sent Me to heal the brokenhearted, to preach deliverance to the captives, and recovery of sight to the blind and to set at liberty them that are bruised."**
> **Luke 4:18 (KJV)**

I don't think we comprehend to the fullest extent how deep the bruise of sexual abuse really goes. BUT GOD goes deeper.

Little girls who have been sexually molested get very mixed up sexually. Many turn to homosexuality. Homosexuality is pervasive in women's prisons. Some call it being "gay for the stay." In other words, they are saying they are not really homosexual, but because they are lonely while incarcerated, they get a girlfriend and have a sexual relationship.

I tell new inmate arrivals at orientation that they don't need a relationship while in prison at all. They should concentrate on healing their relationship with family and children and not concentrate on a partner. I tell them it is not a question of heterosexual or homosexual relationship. They had an unhealthy relationship with a guy on the outside and now an unhealthy relationship with a woman on the inside (prison). Once you are introduced to this type of sexual sin, I don't believe the devil lets go of this yoke in your lives after you get out.

If an inmate gets into serious trouble time and time again at EWCC, they are sent back to a higher security level prison such as Mabel Basset prison, which houses maximum and medium inmates. They don't have the freedom of a minimum-security unit like EWCC. Sometimes, the inmate they had a relationship with will commit some infraction of the rules *on purpose* so they can also be shipped back to Mabel Bassett, and serve more time, because she can't live without her partner! She does not care that these actions can lead to more time in prison—and more time that her kids won't see her. Basically, what these partners are saying with their actions: I love my partner more than I love my kids.

This homosexuality thing is a big deal for volunteers *and* non-homosexual inmates. Inmate-wise, other inmates are always frustrated and judgmental and look down on homosexuals. I don't blame them because not only is it wrong (against God's Word), but they have to hear their sexual activities at night in the dorms. I just tell them I hate that situation and they should not be subjected to that. But I also say that they shouldn't be overly judgmental because though they may not be homosexual themselves, many of them will go out and commit adultery or fornication as quickly as possible soon after they are released!

For volunteers, they want to know if they are permitted to preach against homosexuality in our "politically correct" society. I tell them they can say anything they want if it's in the Bible, but they should also include *all* sexual sin. It wouldn't hurt to preach about homosexuality, fornication and adultery, as sexual sin. This way, they are not just picking on the homosexual.

Lord knows we need some specific preaching on fornication and adultery as well as homosexuality. Over half the church people in the Christian world are living together (unmarried) sexually active, which is just as much a sin as homosexuality. I have had inmates tell me after they got out and went to church: "Chaplain, you told us we should live holy lives and not have sex with anyone until we were married, but we see that living together sexually seems accepted in the churches.'

Shame on us for overlooking sexual sin, by not preaching and teaching about it. Is it because we don't want to lose churchgoers? We are making healthy families obsolete! The *truth* is what sets people free (John 8:32) –not acceptance of a sinful lifestyle. We are so caught up in the

111

homosexuality issue, that we forget about other types of sexual sin.

Women who were molested as little girls may not be in a wheelchair, but they are crippled nonetheless—crippled mentally, emotionally and sexually.

I'm so glad Jesus came to heal those who are broken deep inside.

CHAPTER 10

Abortion Recovery

The abortion recovery class is currently taught by Mary Painter. She takes a very negative situation and turns it into a beautiful, freeing, and very powerful class.

After the first few classes, the attendees, some of whom have had multiple abortions, name and complete a birth certificate with little footprints on them, for each baby they have aborted. The purpose is for every woman to accept the reality of the abortion in their lives.

It is followed with a teaching on self-forgiveness and steps to freedom. The class ends with a candlelight memorial service for each baby not born. It is a beautiful, touching, powerful, and truly freeing class. This is a difficult class to get through and to teach, but it is also POWERFUL!

"For if you embrace the truth, it will release true freedom into your lives".
John 8:32 (TPT)

CHAPTER 11

Codependency/Marriage & Relationships
(or How to Be "Jerk Free")

These two classes are "biggies." Relationships can make or break women. They are ever so important to us; unhealthy ones are devastating.

The "codependency" class illustrates how, we as women, tend to be willing to do what it takes to keep the relationship going. But lines are crossed when we go against what we know to be right and do wrong, wrong, wrong— just to please our "Mr. Yum-Yum."

And we talk a LOT about "Mr. Yum-Yum."

Teaching large classes helps me because I need to say some strong things which, if said to an individual lady would be hurtful. However, when I have a large class, I am able to say things and direct it towards the whole group.

I start these classes with this question: "So, all those casual sexual relationships, how are they working for you? Now we are in a thinking mode. Relationships, relationships, relationships! They really can make or break us. Just how many are tired of being broken?"

Every woman wants to be loved. We've been in LUV with someone once we were five years old, but later, in our efforts to find real LOVE, we settle for everything BUT love. Women can assume that, if we are having sex with a guy and he is staying with us that there is a relationship forming.

I share that most every woman inside or outside of prison has been hooked up with at least one jerk—if not more. We are women in relationships where we wrap our entire identity around Mr. Yum-Yum.

I share a survey of about 200 couples who lived together for at least the past two years. Men [and women] in these relationships were separated from one another and each group was asked: "What do you really think about your live-in relationships? Ninety-four percent of the women said they really *loved* their partner and they got along well, he was good to her kids, and she was committed the relationship long-term.

They asked the men in these same relationships how they felt about their live-in relationship. Ninety-three percent said something to the effect that this current relationship was regular sex and good meals, but they would only hang around until they met their REAL soul mate.

Men don't think about relationships like we do. Welcome to the real world.

We draw a visual demonstration on the dry erase board. The women taking the class tell me the reasons why they get into relationships at all. As they shout out such reasons as: loneliness; financial help; help with my kids; etc. Of course, I write at the top of the board "sex." Then I begin a discussion with them asking how each one of these reasons look *after the guy leaves*, because they do eventually leave.

Did they give you help with your loneliness? No, not really. They say are lonelier than ever. I erase *that* reason to get into a relationship off the board.

Did they help you with your kids? No, the kids caused lots of arguments and they were definitely NOT helpful with their kids. I erase "help with the kids."

Did they help you out financially? No, they reply they are worse off financially because they were paying *his* bills. I erase that reason off the board.

I ask how they feel sexually after Mr. Yum-Yum leaves? They reply they feel used and just something the guy can toss away. I erase that reason for having a relationship.

Soon we have a blank board. I point out that this is what you have now after they leave. *None* of the things you really wanted from a relationship are there.

I point out that their kids are affected negatively, too—by all these guys who come and go in their lives. Even if the guy who stayed with you for a while never paid any attention to the kids, in the kid's minds—they think, the guy left "us." They feel the rejection.

And I don't want to hear about "baby-daddy." He may have made the baby, but he "ain't no Daddy." Real fathers stay and take responsibility for their babies. I also say that not one of them in the room EVER wants anything to happen to their children but look at the 6:00p.m. news. Who shakes babies? Kills babies? Molests kids? Boyfriends in the home. It is our responsibility to put our children before our boyfriends, before our own loneliness. God will honor you and take care of you and your children, if you act honorably.

So, here is Mr. Yum-Yum, doing what he wants for as long as he wants and leaving when he wants. Then we discuss our choices. Why would you want a guy who is 40 years old and still living with his mom? Why do you want a guy who can't keep or doesn't have a job? Let's stop and think about what we are getting into...

I share that during my 47- year marriage, my husband and I argued way too much. In a real marriage relationship,

119

you don't wake up every morning just "slappy happy." But no matter how mad my husband got at me; he NEVER raised a hand to even act like he was going to hit me. It gets really quiet in the class. Usually, at least one lady will tell me that she was told by her mom that its ok for the guy to hit you as long as it doesn't get "too bad." (I don't know what "too bad" means.) They were also told they could not make it without a man in their house and that, even if he went out on you, as long as he brings home his paycheck, it was ok. I tell them "You are each worth more than that. He may bring home more than his paycheck: like a sexually transmitted disease (STD)."

I don't ask for raised hands, but I ask how many grew up seeing their mom in a relationship with someone who drinks, drugs and/or beats mom up? How many of you said to yourself, "I never want to be with a man like that?" Then how many of you went right out and hooked up with some guy just like that?" It's because that is what you accept as "normal," even though it's not right.

We discuss how difficult relationships are to maintain in the world in which we live. I point out it's not only because they are incarcerated that they can't seem to maintain (or ever find) a good relationship. Movie stars are beautiful, rich, educated, etc., but how are *their* relationships working out? They reply, "Not too well. They live with someone and then they break up numerous times. So, it's a challenge for *anyone* to find and maintain a good, Godly relationship.

Then we discuss our little "side relationships" with our "Sugar Daddies" while we are incarcerated. We maintain correspondence with them saying what sexy fun we are going to have with them when we get out of prison—as long as they keep sending us money. Yet you have no intention of being with them when you get out. You are using them, the way men have used you. I point out that maintaining this type of relationship is just prostitution through the mail. I don't know why, but I never get applause after that statement.

Sometimes when an inmate has maintained her sugar daddy relationship in prison and she is finally discharged, she passes his address on to another inmate who is going to be incarcerated for a while. Then he starts sending money and talking about a relationship with the new inmate. Once, a guy called me to say he knew that his name was passed down to other inmates about three times, but he said, "Chaplain, I really think the one I'm corresponding with now is the one."

Another time, a really snooty lawyer called me from New York. He explained that his client's grown children were upset and worried because their 75-year-old father, who was quite wealthy, had been corresponding with an inmate at Eddie Warrior. He had sent her and her grown children lots of his money in anticipation of her getting out of prison and coming to live with him. I asked the lawyer how I could help him? Dripping with sarcasm, he said in a distinctly condescending voice, "Well, don't you all 'down there in Oklahoma' have any laws against this?" I replied, "No, do you all 'up there in New York' have any laws against an elderly man being stupid?" He hung up.

We talk about how we get into relationships and that honestly, after they get out, they should not hook up with anyone for at last a year, if not two to give them a chance to make sure they are going to make it. They moan, "What? A year?"

I tell them I've never seen a tombstone that said, "Died for Lack of Sex."

We discuss codependent relationships and how men try to control us by "gaslighting" (making us think we are crazy), or by "intimate terrorism" (what goes on in the bedroom against our will). *No one talks about this, but it is common in codependent relationships.*

Here are some examples of codependency:

• She is so worried about Mr. Yum-Yum even though he beat her up so badly she ended up in the hospital. She was really worried and felt bad for him because he probably really hurt his hands when he used his fists to put a hole in the door, in order to get to her to beat her up. She felt bad about him hurting his hands.

• A slightly older lady came to my office crying so hard between words that I could barely understand her. She choked, "Chaplain, I need to make an emergency call to my husband. I'm so worried about him." I asked if he were in the hospital or on hospice. She said he was home, but she was so worried about him because he has had heart trouble

123

in the past. I said I didn't quite understand. She continued crying and said, " I'm just worried about him because he has had heart problems and his girlfriend is in the hospital and I'm worried about him because I know he is worried about her."

• One of the inmate chapel clerks would call her husband at home and he would yell and cuss at her the whole time they were on the phone. Then, she would come to work at the chapel crying. I watched this happen over and over, again and again. Finally, I said "Why do you continue to call your husband when you know he is going to upset you by calling you names and cussing you out?" She said, "Well, chaplain, I only call him so he can send me some money while I'm in here. As soon as I get out, I'm going to leave him.

I told her she could certainly do what she wanted, but if you depend on him for money while you are incarcerated, then when you get out, you will go to him for money. You need to make God your source, not an abusive husband. I understand about wanting money, but you need to decide now who your source is: God or Mr. Yum-Yum?

• Another woman's story: At 17, running from a horrible home life, she met a guy about 35 years old, a thief, doing drugs, etc. Someone was killed while she was with him during a drug deal. He quickly told her that if she would take the blame, she would only get a year or two because she was so young. He also pointed out how much he loved her and that, if he were convicted of the crime he would probably have to spend 10-20 years in prison and he could not stand to be away from her for that long because he *really* loved her. She bought it. She said that even the jailers told her again and again that this guy was using her and she should not take the blame for the crime. But she was in love with him and didn't want to be away from him. She went to court. Guess who was the first witness against her in her case? Yep, Mr. Yum-Yum. She served 14 years in prison.

• An ex-inmate chapel clerk hooked up with a particular Mr. Yum-Yum. She said she was not doing drugs, but he was. She had been attending a particular church. People in that church "prophesied" over her that this guy was God's will for her: God's man for her. Just because a guy is in church doesn't mean he is healed. You know, most of us come to Jesus pretty messed up. Someone can be genuinely saved, but not well or whole yet. Well sure

125

enough, he was in church, then out, then in, then out: and on drugs. She called me to say she didn't know exactly what to do. She said she was not doing drugs and he was trying to get off drugs.

Mr. Yum-Yum is always "trying." I told her that if he was on and off drugs that was not the man God wanted for her. She said they weren't having sex, but he was crashing on her couch. I told her it wouldn't be long before he went from her couch to her bed. I told her when he leaves next time, put his belongings on the front porch and lock the door and file a restraining order. She didn't listen. She is back on drugs.

I don't really mean to be mean, but when an ex-inmate calls me, I have this one window of opportunity to be straight with her: to tell her the whole truth. It might be the difference in her getting her thinking straight or going down the tubes.

I have also had several good reports from these relationships' classes. One ex-inmate told me she started to hook up with a couple of guys when she first got out and it just never seemed to work out. Then she was allowed visitation with her nine-year-old son and before she knew it, DHS wanted to restore her rights to her son since she had worked steadily, had an apartment and was stable. She said, "It was the funniest thing, chap, it was just me and my son and I have never been so happy and free. It's the first time I didn't have a man in my house. It's the first time in my life if I want to buy my son some jeans, I don't have to ask anyone's permission. I don't want to be without anyone all my life, but for now, it feels good just to be *me* and *my son*."

I ran into another ex-inmate at a department store. She looked great and was grinning from car to ear. She was quick to tell me that when I taught the relationship class, she thought I was crazy to teach us to wait to have sex until marriage. She said that this guy she met had many other women in the past and she had other men, but they decided they really loved each other and wanted to wait and honor God. I asked her if she was happy. She said "We are both like young kids—waiting to have sex until marriage. We are getting married in two months and we are both so happy."

God's way works! He knows a little bit about sex – He invented it. I do have a few questions to ask him about when I get to heaven though!

127

A Real Man

I point out that a real man will want what's best for you. My husband never went to college. I have my master's degree and guess who my biggest fan is? Yes, my husband. He is not trying to control me but encourages me to do what I feel God would have me do. He is proud of me.

I shared with the ladies that one day I asked my dad if he enjoyed working for the telephone company. He had worked 30 years for them and retired. He looked puzzled. I don't know what you mean, sis? I needed a job because I was young with a young family. I never worried about whether I liked it or not.

People used to put responsibility and doing the right thing ahead of their personal happiness. Now it seems to be the other way around.

I share with the inmates some things that I went through in my 47 years of marriage. One was the trip my husband and I made to Galveston, Texas. This was known by the chapel clerks as "Chaplain's Galveston Story."

One weekend when we were about 60 years old, we went to the beach at Galveston. My hubby and I were both sitting in beach chairs and looking around. Then began the parade of young women who probably weighed about 90 pounds, they were all marching right in front of us in their little bikinis. I looked at them and for a moment felt kind of sad. I said to the Lord, 'I could work out 24/7 for the next year and *never* look like those girls.' They were in their bikinis, and I was trying to grab all my upper leg cellulite to fit it *into* my one-piece bathing suit. I thought, "I really *am* old. My husband was trying to keep from looking too much at the girls as *they* passed by. He looked at me for a moment, and it was as if he knew what I was thinking. He said, "Kathey, you know, of course, you are the most beautiful woman on this beach."

I point out to the ladies in the class that my husband still loved me after all the years we had been together—even though I had "furniture disease." You all know what "furniture disease" is, don't you? It's when your chest falls down to your drawers.

I saw one of the inmates who had taken this class after she had been out of prison about six years. She reminded me of my "Galveston story" and said when I shared it, she immediately told God— "God, I want a man to love me just like Chaplain's husband loved her *and* I want to drive a truck." She said, "I just added the truck because I had been thinking about what I wanted to do when I got out of prison. Guess what chaplain? I met a guy who is crazy about me, and we have been married three years and—I drive a truck."

I am quick to point out to the other inmates that she did not meet this guy until she had been out about three years. She lived to tell about it. I point out to the women taking the class that most all the women I know who were released from prison had to wait two or three years before they met the man God wanted them to marry. They didn't die either.

We have power points: pointing out the things to look for in a man that will be an indication of whether he is a good bet or a bad bet? Why doesn't a 40-year-old Mr. Yum-Yum have a place to live? Why can't he get or keep a job? Does he blame everyone else for his problems? Is he hot-tempered? Does he feel sorry for himself all the time?

Every woman with children *wants* to be able to go back to Mr. Yum-Yum and live happily ever after with him and the kids. But, as I said before, Mr. Yum-Yum is *always* "trying." Don't misunderstand—it would be wonderful *if* he would do some things to prove his good intentions like completing a Parenting class, seeing a counselor, etc. There are all kinds of free programs out there he could take to verify his sincere attempt to make things better for his wife and children. Mr. Yum-Yum always has the "words" for reconciliation—but not the actions.

The ladies who take this class say it's a good one because it isn't really complicated, and the simple truths it illuminated were eye-opening.

CHAPTER 12

Parenting From Prison

"Parenting From Prison" is exactly that: How to be a good mom from prison.

This class points out that no one says you don't love your children or that your children don't love you. It's not a love issue: it's a trust issue.

Our families and kids love us—they just don't trust us. You can tell them all day long that you have changed, but they will not be impressed until you have walked it out in front of them—not just talked about it. It took time to lose their trust—and it will take some time to earn their trust back.

Studies show that children worry about their mothers. They worry about them being mistreated. And, as much as they really want Mom to come home and hug and kiss them, they may not be able to verbalize it, but in the back of their little minds, they are afraid that when you get out of prison, you will take them back to where they came from before you were sent to prison.

We talk about writing home. What not to write: how awful it is. What to write: about you taking a new class or obtaining your GED or getting your hair cut, etc., and ask about *them*—not only about what's going on with you. We talk about training—not solely discipline. Love, affirmation and healing our relationships with our children is emphasized in the "want to" and explicitly in the "how to."

Inmates must assure their children that when they get out of prison, they are not going to go directly to where they are and jerk them out of where they are. This is not fair to the kids, especially if they are doing well where they are living. And inmates need to be sure they can make it out there: get a job; a place to live; etc.

It's also about older as well as younger children. It's about clarifying your expectations and not just threatening your children all the time and yelling at them but taking time to talk with them. Set realistic boundaries and consequences and make those consequences known.

Example: Two young boys go to toy store to buy something with money given to them by their grandparents. One throws a fit and says he's not buying a toy. His little brother is fine with buying a toy with his money. Mom and Dad explain that if he doesn't buy a toy today, they won't be back for two weeks. He still behaves stubbornly. Imagine that?! He refuses to buy a toy. His parents explain to him again that if he continues this behavior, he will not be able to buy a toy for two weeks, but also, he will not be allowed to play with his little brother's toy at all during that time. Still, he refuses.

So, guess what? When he gets home, he starts crying and says he is sorry and begs to go back to the toy store. Should his parents take him back? Our discussion turns to saying what you mean and meaning what you say and reminding the young boy that they explained what the consequences were. Should they take him back to the store? No spanking, screaming, or threatening took place. This was good training. It's not always just a matter of spanking and staying frustrated.

As far as teenagers are concerned, the best way to handle them is to lock them in a closet from the time they are 13 until they are 20. Of course, you should give them food and water....!!

One inmate told me she once sent home a little "I love you" note to her 14-year-old son. Well, you and I know that he's not going to say much about it—he's a 14-year-old boy. When she asked if he got it, he said, "Yeah". And that was that. But at Visiting Day at the prison a few months later, a small, tattered piece of paper fell out of his pocket during his visit. It was her note. He had kept it with him. So, even though all she got was a "yeah", it meant something to him.

One inmate told me her 13-year-old daughter was furious at her for being incarcerated, she would not talk to her when she called home and NEVER replied to her letters. However, one day mom wrote her a note that said, "I am taking a parenting class to try to learn how to be a better mother."

For the first time in two years, her daughter wrote back and said, "That's good, Mom." That might not seem

135

like much, but to her it was wonderful. We discuss not waiting six or seven weeks and then sending our kids a "purge" letter about how sorry we are, and it wasn't how it was meant to be, etc. Instead, write a short, light-content letter once a week. Consistency builds trust.

One inmate told me she had two little girls ages three and five. She would always send one letter to both of them. She said after she took the parenting class, she decided that even though her three-year-old couldn't read at all, she would send her a letter each week just for her. The grandmother who was taking care of the girls said that even though the little one couldn't read, she recognized the handwriting on the letter, expected it every week and when it arrived, she wouldn't even let grandmother read it. She would just grab it, run to her room and put it under her pillow.

Caregivers. Wow. They are wonderful and usually not appreciated by the inmate moms whose children they care for. I suggest instead of pressuring their families to send *them* money, to send a couple of dollars to the caregivers. Most caregivers are family and are usually grandmother and grandfather.

And of course, the inmates say they will only concentrate on their children upon release, but when they get out "Mr. Yum-Yum" is the person they want to please and minister to—not their children. This must be addressed: A decision must be made.

We talk about the power of our words. The old rhyme, "Sticks and Stones can break my bones, but words can never hurt me." We discuss how this is not true.

Their children *need* kind words. They have been broken in many areas of their lives and it's not unusual for children of inmates to have mental and emotional problems, as a result.

> **"Anxious fear brings depression, but a life-giving word of encouragement can do wonders to restore joy to the heart."**
> **Proverbs 12:25 (TPT)**

Children also act out what is "modeled" in front of them—right or wrong. They watch what you do. They see what you value and what you don't value. Sometimes we need to take stock of who we "admire", like a renown athlete or a movie star. We sometimes admire someone who is worth millions but has the character of a worm.

For example, if a woman who is a bartender gets saved, we would tell her that she really needs to leave that environment and change what she does for a living, no matter how hard that may be for her now that she is saved.

But, if she is an actor or actress, we would not think of telling her that now that she is saved, she should no longer make movies that use the "F" word and display nudity in the movies they star in. They would probably respond saying, "Well, that's my job—I'm an actor." Never mind the fact that we feel the woman working in a bar should change her life—even though she has limited skills. But the actress is rich enough to live the rest of her life luxuriously on what she has already made.

We have to be careful we are not sending the message to our kids that if you're wealthy, you can do anything you want with your life, but if you are someone less fortunate, we expect you to make righteous choices.

"So that you may surely learn to sense what is vital, and approve and prize what is excellent and of real value, recognizing the highest and the best, and distinguishing the moral Differences..."

Philippians 1:10 (AMP)

Character is to be valued more than money.

If you receive a welfare check, that's fine, but don't be lazy. Be a good mom. Make sure your children have a decent breakfast before they leave for school; even if it's just gravy and a biscuit or bread. Then, make sure your place is clean. Clean sheets, clean furniture, clean clothes. Be there when they get home. Try to create a place for them to do their homework. Fix them a hot meal, even if it's only hotdogs. Don't spend all day on your phone or computer. Be a mom.

Female inmates have often already lost custody of their children before they come to prison, or they lose custody while in prison. They say that DHS took their kids from them. I don't mean to be harsh, but I tell them DHS did not take your kids: *your* choices and behavior took them. DHS does not want your kids. They don't even have a place for them. I tell them DHS is not the enemy. They are directed to write to their DHS workers once a month, and let them know about the classes they are taking. They should also ask DHS if there is anything they can do to help their children.

Sometimes their children have already been adopted. If this is the case, the inmates always pray for an "open adoption." A "closed adoption", is of course, just that: The inmate may never know who adopted their children or where they live. An "open adoption" is when the adoptive parents allow an inmate limited contact with their children through the adoptive parents. In some cases, the children are older and already know who their mom is and want to talk with her.

Interesting story: An inmate came into my office and said, "Chaplain, I was praying about my kids, and I felt that God would have me ask you to pray and agree with me that I will find where my children are and will be allowed limited contact with them through their adoptive parents. I asked what she knew about the situation. She stated that it was a closed adoption, and she thought her children were living out of state in one of the five states surrounding Oklahoma. Outside of that, she knew nothing. I told her I would agree with her, but that, God was going to have to do some things to find these people, since she had virtually no knowledge of where to start. I really had to stretch my faith to agree with her, but I told her I would. So we prayed.

I didn't hear from her for about three months. Then she burst into my office with tears streaming down her cheeks and a smile on her face. "Guess what?" she said, "I received a letter from the people who had adopted all three of my kids. They said they had been trying to find me for a few months. They told me they really love my kids, but that since they are moving into their teens, they started mentioning me and had prayed about how to handle this situation.

The Lord helped them to find me; they started their search three months ago. Chaplain, they actually felt it would be best for the kids to have limited contact with me! I told them our Chap said never to undermine adoptive parents' role because they have been doing what we *should* have been doing: taking care of our kids. They even gave me their phone number and allowed me to write one letter a month (if I keep it positive) and call once a month. Hallelujah! I just love Jesus!" With tears in her eyes, she said, "I wish I could hug you Chaplain." (Hugging is not allowed).

Many times, inmates will ask me to pray that they will get custody of their children when they get out. I tell them honestly that I cannot in good conscience pray that. I ask them if they want the best for their children: God's Will. They always say "Yes." Then I say, then let's pray for God's Will to be done in the lives of our children. After all, inmates don't really know if they can make it on the outside yet. They need some time outside of prison to see how they are going to navigate life.

I had one inmate who got mad at me for even suggesting that she wouldn't make it after she got out and that she missed her kids and was going directly from prison to get them. She returned to prison a year or so afterward and came to my office. She said that much as she hated to admit it, she headed straight toward her kids at her mom's house, but she said, "Chaplain, I met one of my old drug dealers in my neighborhood and I was high about three hours after I left Eddie Warrior. I'm so glad I didn't make it to pick them up and take them out of where they were."

Parenting From Prison Class is a requirement to participate in "Play Day."

CHAPTER 13

Play Day

Play Days are a really big thing at Eddie Warrior Correctional Center.

Play Day is when an inmate can spend a good part of a day with only her children. Not even caregivers are allowed in. Of course, there are numerous consent forms that must be filled out and signed by the Legal Guardian to give their permission for this to take place. Play Days take place only in the Gym and the playground. Volunteers are present and oversee and keep an eye on everything.

Play Day is a privilege, not a right. It is earned. Inmates who wish to attend must have (1) completed the "Parenting from Prison" class, and (2) must have no misconducts or incident reports in the last six months prior a Play Day, and (3) their children's Legal Guardians have to permit it.

The inmates sometimes ask why they have to jump through so many hoops to participate in Play Day. I tell them, it doesn't take very long to make a baby, it takes a little longer to have a baby, but it takes a lifetime of right decisions to raise a child. Some complain, but most of the inmate ladies will do *anything* required to make this happen. They want to see their kids.

Play Days happen three times per year: Fall Break, Spring Break and Summer. Church vans from Oklahoma City, Tulsa, and Lawton bring kids to EWCC to be with their inmate Moms. Of course, the vans also have consent forms for them that must be filled out and signed by the Legal Guardian of the children.

Thank God for the "van volunteers." For years, they never miss a beat and bring vans full of kids EVERY Play Day. They are amazing.

Please understand that I am *not* saying they need to get their kids back or even have access to their children's lives. They need to prove to themselves and to others that they can be trusted with their kids. Some will never get their kids back, *but* studies say that kids do better, in school and at home, if they are allowed to have limited contact with their inmate moms. It gives them peace of mind to see that mom is ok and (I really emphasize again), that they know that Mom is not just going to get out and jerk them up from where they are and take them with her anywhere. It also gives the children peace if the inmate shows respect and appreciation towards the caregiver.

For Play Day, we have face paints, pizza, games, balls, and pictures are taken of Mom and kids. It's a very productive day. The inmates think it's for them and, of course, it is great for them, but it's *really* for the kids.

Three Chiefs of Security have told me that Play Days are real Visiting Days because they are productive. They say that most of the time, at regular visiting for family, Mr. Yum-Yum brings the kids, but the inmate mom focuses most of her time flirting with her Mr. Yum-Yum. At Play Day, they only see their kids.

Children of inmates are referred to as "at risk" kids. This is because statistically, they are at a higher risk of ending up in prison themselves. I have several inmates who were serving time at EWCC—so were their moms—at the same time.

Play Day and the Reading Programs contribute greatly to the term we at EWCC prefer to use: "Children of Promise" instead of "at-risk kids."

Greg Breslin assigned me to oversee Play Day when he was my boss, and I have forgiven him. I really love it; it's worth the trouble. I expanded it from about 20 kids to 140 kids on Play Day. We had to break it into two days instead of one as it grew. Kids *want* to see *their* mom.

We serve pizza at Play Day. Leave it up to some inmates (not all) to try to do something sneaky, even at a Play Day. I have learned something new every Play Day for the last 20 years.

One Play Day, I discovered that inmates who were helping serve pizza were putting untouched pizzas in the trash bags that would subsequently be picked up by the inmates working in Maintenance. This was their way of getting the pizza to inmates not working Play Day! I discovered this and from then on, I had the volunteers watch closely and be sure that every pizza box that was thrown away was torn in half—with no pizza in it.

One of the next Play Days, I found out that inmates attending Play Day were stuffing pizza slices into their underwear after they had been searched and handing it out to their inmate friends back on their dorms! Well, I would have to really want pizza to eat it after it had been in another inmate's panties.

One Play Day, a grandmother brought her three grandchildren to drop them off for the day; I could see she was really nervous about it. I assured her that there would be plenty of volunteers and some officers walking around and the kids would have pizza, face paints, games, etc. She fought tears and said she was just worried about them. She said the kids were *so* looking forward to it. I told her that she could leave them, drive into Muskogee, take herself out to dinner, shop at a mall and then maybe take in a movie. Just relax. She hesitated, but said, "Ok."

When the next Play Day rolled around, there she was! I recognized her and said I was glad to see her back and said hopefully it wouldn't be so hard for her. She smiled and said, "Hard?" I could hardly wait to bring them back. I did what you said and had a blast just being by myself for once." Yay!

We always had an Easter Egg hunt at the Play Days during Spring Break. We had Halloween candy bags on Fall Break. It was just a good day. I always prayed for no rain— only good weather for the Play Days. And, honestly, in the 20 years I have done Play Day, I can only remember around 12 times that the weather didn't cooperate. It was really a good day to see the smiles on the kids' faces every Play Day. It really was a "healing time" for the kids and their moms.

It takes about six weeks, 30 faithful volunteers AND about 25 aspirin to get ready for a Play Day. It's a big undertaking. And worth it.

One inmate visited my office. She was laughing. She said, "Chap, I called home to tell my 10-year-old daughter that I was being released, but before I could get that out, my daughter said she was *really* looking forward to Play Day because it was so much fun. She went on to say, "I told her that we wouldn't be doing Play Day because I was *getting out and coming home*. There was a silence from my daughter. I was so excited, but it didn't seem like she was. There was silence. Then she said, "Yes, Mom, I'm glad you are coming home, but can I just go to Play Day without you? It's so much fun!!

Another time, I was leading a volunteer orientation off-site and one of the new volunteers said her 18-year-old daughter wanted to say something to me and the others who were being trained to do volunteer work. She came up to the front of the room and was fighting tears. She said if it had not been for Play Days, she would never have seen or had a relationship with her mom who was an inmate there at Eddie Warrior. She said, "My grandmother could not bring me to Play Days. Without the availability of the vans from Oklahoma City bringing me, I would never have seen my mom from the time I was 12-16 years old. But because of Play Day and the faithfulness of the volunteers who helped make it happen, I was able to see my Mom and it made a difference in my life. Thank you, Chaplain and thank you volunteers."

Well, there wasn't a dry eye in the house, and I thought – so, Lord, it *really* is worth the work to make it happen. Thank you.

One little boy was talking to me after Play Day. We were waiting for his grandparents to pick him up. I asked him if he had a good time and he said he did. He liked seeing his mom, but his voice rose and said, "Yes, that's my mom, but as long as she doesn't keep her act together, and do the right thing, I'm staying with my grandparents. They are my parents." He seemed like he was eight years old, going on 20. He was such a likeable kid, and over the years, I saw him grow up seeing his mom, but truly loving and appreciating his grandparents. I liked him, because once he asked me how old I was. I said, "How old do you think I am?" He studied me for a minute and then said, "I think you are about 20 years old." Being 66, I said, "Yes, that's right" –someone go get this kid another piece of pizza!

Several years ago, our wonderful volunteer from the Lawton area brought several kids to see their moms on Play Day. It was a 5-hour drive each way to bring kids to Play Day. One particular inmate who worked in the Chapel, had three kids. All three were struggling with issues and she was doing her best to change all that. The kid who really stood out was her 12-year-old son. He had about the *worst* attitude *ever*! For about five years the faithful volunteer drove in for Play Day. She could have refused to bring him to each Play

Day because of his attitude, but she was determined to bring these kids, with all their problems, to be with their mom on Play Day. Then, they missed a few Play Days.

Years passed, then lo and behold, a young man about 16 years old jumped out of the Lawton van, ran to me as I was checking kids in for Play Day and gave me the biggest hug. He said he was *so glad* to see me; he almost had tears in his eyes, except that he was also smiling *so big* at me! It was the twelve-year-old boy – now 16. He said he wanted to thank me for doing Play Day.

Come to find out, this volunteer not only wanted to help the children, but even helped the inmate when she got out. She said God had instructed her to concentrate on *this* family. She helped the inmate get a house and she went on to help her complete her college degree. I didn't know it, but all those years, the volunteer had the three kids in counseling, and showed them no nonsense, but consistent love and patience.

The volunteer was amazing. The kids were amazing. And the inmate mom was amazing in the way she handled her kids and put them first in all her prayers, and her actions towards them. Most of all—God was amazing! As always! Change is hard to gauge and many times it takes more than a few months, even a few years to get the eggs unscrambled, but with God, all things *are* possible.

Play Day is not the only special program that inmates at Eddie Warrior were allowed to participate in to help their kids.

CHAPTER 14

Reading Programs for Kids

In addition to Play Day, another special and very important reading program is called "MOM'S TOUCH." This reading program is designed to help inmates read a book on CD to their children. We send the book, with Mom's voice recorded reading the book and a picture of Mom to their children.

Volunteers packed the envelopes for security purposes and donate postage for them to be sent to inmates' kids.

Of course, the Legal Guardian has to send us a Consent form to allow us to send it to the kids before they can participate.

A compassionate volunteer who was a wife of one of our officers heard about this program and got local businesswomen together to launch it. She obtained a grant for funding and her team went through volunteer training and came in once a month to do about 50 of these "Mom's Touch" recordings.

Chaplains from the men's facilities have the same program for the men, but there is far less participation. We have about 60 inmates wanting to do this and a long waiting list. Male inmates simply don't participate as much at the men's facilities. They have to ask: "WHICH KIDS?" They have "fathered" many kids as they went from bed to bed sleeping with numerous women. One male inmate at another facility bragged that he had fathered over 18 kids when he was "sowing his wild oats." He had nothing to brag about—animals can do that.

Sorry, don't mean to be so harsh, because women are responsible, too, but all this "messing around" causes a big mess. *You* become a mess and the lives of the children you have created become a mess. Stop it! Be a real man or woman of character for the sake of your children.

The Messages Program is another reading program, like Mom's Touch, but instead of sending the kids a CD with Mom's voice on it, they are able to create a DVD of their inmate mom to send to their children. The wonderful volunteers who facilitate this great program come twice a year: once at Christmas and once in time for Mother's Day.

Once I received a phone call from a caregiver from Iowa. She said that when she first received a "Consent Form" she had to fill out to get permission for her four-year-old grandson to receive a DVD from his inmate Mom. She said, "Honestly, I thought who cares about a DVD? I just need my daughter to get out of prison and live right and do right by her son. But, Chaplain, ever since my grandson had received this DVD, not only has he had more peace, but he makes me play the DVD of Mom almost every day and every time, he goes up to the TV screen and kisses his mom on the screen. Chaplain, thank you. Being so young, I didn't think it would make any kind of difference to him   but it has. He is now a much happier kid. I didn't really realize how much he missed his mom.

CHAPTER 15

Victory Bible College

We are blessed as a facility to have a program that most staff members agree with and allow inmates who qualify to attend: Victory Bible College. Victory Church in Tulsa sponsors the curriculum. I have seen it change so many lives.

This is a year-long program and is considered a full-time job for those 25 inmates who qualify for this Bible College. The criteria for inmates to participate in VBC is the same as the criteria for someone outside of prison.

When my husband and I attended Victory Bible College many years ago (outside of prison), we made friends with others entering ministry. But for several years after we graduated, most all of those who had been in classes with us had ministry positions somewhere. We, however, were both still working secular jobs. I prayed about this many times:

Lord, I know we are called to ministry. Why does everyone else we graduated with have ministry positions? God didn't answer at first, but I kept asking. Finally, I felt an impression: "You and Bobby are called to ministry, but you have to let your character catch up with your anointing." I knew this was true and just might be true for the women at EWCC who attended this powerful Bible College.

"The entrance and unfolding of your Word gives light; their unfolding gives understanding, discernment and comprehension to the simple."
Psalms 119:130 (AMP)

"Break open your Word within me until Revelation light shines out."
Psalms 119:130 (TPT)

"Take My yoke upon you and come and LEARN of me, for I am meek and lowly in heart and you shall find rest unto your souls. For My yoke is easy and My burden is light."
Matthew 11:29 (KJV)

"For this reason we also from the day we heard of it, have not ceased to pray and make special request for you, asking that you may be filled with the full, deep and clear knowledge of His will in all spiritual wisdom, In comprehensive insight into the ways

> **and purposes of God, and in understanding and discernment of spiritual things."**
> **Colossians 1:9 (AMP)**

During the time the women attend VBC, they nearly all feel that God has a particular ministry for them after they are released from prison. Of course, I encourage them to listen for God's voice for direction in their lives. I also emphasize that if they never obtain all they believe God wants them to do, that a life lived for God brings Glory to Him.

> **"I have no greater joy than this, to hear that my spiritual children are living their lives in the Truth."**
> **III John 1:4 (AMP)**

I tell the inmates enrolled to "think spiritually." That is, to weigh what they are taught and begin to develop their spiritual life.

Volunteers from Victory Church sponsor and oversee VBC. Founding Pastor of Victory Church, Pastor Sharon Daugherty, who is very busy, makes the time to host the graduations, complete with caps and gowns. It is really a positive course of study.

The Word is renewing the minds of the women who attend VBC as it is deepening their relationship with Him. I am so thankful for Victory Bible College.

CHAPTER 16

Christian Women's Association (CWA)

Christian Women's Association (CWA) was founded by Leo Brown. He had the vision for it—and I "watered it" and helped it grow. Everything has a small beginning and CWA is no exception. It started small, with about 25 inmates joining it and now it has grown to over 250 inmates. CWA, of course, stresses and recognizes as its guideline – the Word of God. There is a President, Vice-President, Treasurer, Secretary, etc. It is an inmate church organization and issues are discussed and voted on in their monthly meetings. It is run like any organization and teaches responsibility, character, order and accountability. These are valuable teachings for anything we do in life. They facilitate two church services monthly.

Occasionally, CWA ladies in this particular club say they will be glad when they can get out and go to a real church where there is no strife. I tell them "Good luck with that." Even the occasional unrest and strife and learning how to deal with such things, are a part of both church and secular life.

They work on Play Days to serve food and to clean the Gym after the Play Day. They have an attitude of "make me a blessing – even here"! They are quick to respond anytime the Chapel has a need.

About twice a year, Volunteer Mary facilitates a foot washing service for the leaders of CWA. They are ministered to and honored for their servants' attitude and faithfulness.

> **"After that He poureth water into a basin, and began to wash the disciples' feet and to wipe them with the towel with which He was girded.**
> **John 13:5 (KJV)**
>
> **If I then, your Lord and Master have washed your feet; ye also ought to wash one another's feet."**
> **John 13:14 (KJV)**

We don't do this often, but when we do, it is really spiritually powerful.

CWA helps members develop spiritually in their gifts and callings. Members are given a chance to share or preach. And Christian conduct is always stressed. Even if we have to deal with a member of CWA who is doing something not reflected in God's Word, they do not kick someone out of the organization. They sit down with them and hear what the inmate has to say about the problem. They mercifully pray with the person struggling and put them on probation, so they have time to pray about what decision they want to make to keep from getting dropped from CWA.

> **"Brethen, if any person is overtaken in misconduct or sin of any sort, you who are spiritual, who are responsive to and controlled by the Spirit should set him right and restore and reinstate him, without any sense of superiority and with all gentleness, keeping an attentive eye on yourself, lest you should be tempted also."**
> **Galatians 6:1 (AMP)**

CWA brought forth, supports and manages the following groups:

- Chapel Choir
- Chapel Drama Team
- Chapel Praise Team
- Chapel Intercessory Prayer
- Chapel "Signs & Wonders" (Sign language to religious songs – it's beautiful).

CWA helps fund Play Days and helps with donations for Holiday Gift Bags.

Leadership opportunities are experienced for the first time in most of inmates' lives. This is a really big deal to the inmate members of CWA. They take it seriously and are proud to be a part of it. Some inmates drop out because they don't want to be accountable to *anyone* for their behavior.

The biggest, most overused, used out of context phrase, "Don't Judge Me" is usually the reply from the inmate who is exhibiting behavior that goes against the Word of God. They want to make someone else feel bad for telling the truth about their problem. We don't judge you—that's God's job, but we are accountable to hold *you* accountable. "Don't Judge me". Translation: "I know what

I'm doing is wrong, but I don't want to be held accountable or have someone disagree with me."

> **"Our iniquities, our secret heart and its sins which we would so like to conceal even from ourselves, You have set in the revealing light of Your countenance."**
> **Psalms 90:8 (AMP)**

CWA is a tangible presence on the yard and so respected that other inmates ask members to pray for them personally. And they do.

CHAPTER 17

The Card Shop

Inmates have access to the Canteen for food, snacks, basic school supplies, etc., but the Card Shop is different.

The Card Shop was NOT started by me—surpise! But Mary and I helped it grow. Mary oversaw it more than I did. She was its sponsor and helped the inmates who worked there with inventory, stocking, and general management. Excellent training for life on the "outside."

The Card Shop stocked colored pens, fancy folders, stickers for inmate moms to put on their letters to their kids, coloring books to send to their kids and a more extensive stock of supplies for Education students.

It was started to generate income for Play Day, but as it grew over the years, it not only enabled us to facilitate the growing number of children participating in Play Day, but we supported six children overseas and we give generously to the Women's Shelter in a nearby town.

The shelter managers have told us over the years how much they appreciated our support. The average woman who goes to the shelter goes back to Mr. Yum-Yum, then back to the shelter, then back to Mr. Yum-Yum an average of eight times before they finally make the break from an abusive situation.

We also save our Programs area of the Department of Corrections hundreds of dollars by purchasing the Relationship class books out of Card Shop funds. Since we have so many different things inmates can buy out of their personal account, inmates love to shop there.

Remember: You can take the woman out of the mall, but you can't take the mall out of the woman! We are *gonna* SHOP!

CHAPTER 18

Christmas at Eddie Warrior

Christmas is a difficult time for incarcerated women. It's right up there with "Mother's Day" (THE most difficult day). Women who are incarcerated are fully aware of what their behavior and choices have done to their children. They may or may not be working to improve their behavior, but these are still tough days for them.

So, we have fun at EWCC at Christmas time. We make sure we have a couple of Christmas choirs come in to sing Christmas songs and CWA goes caroling to each dorm during this time. Volunteers (there they go again) contribute to make good Holiday Gift Bags to give all 800 inmates. Money from the Card Shop enables us to purchase gift bags and fill them with allowed items such as: ink pens; writing pads; individually wrapped pieces of candy; candy canes;

greeting cards to send home to family for different occasions; toothpaste and other items.

CWA takes money out of their budgets to buy each inmate a bottle of shampoo and a bottle of conditioner at Christmas.

But one thing they prize above all else is for Christmas is: SOFT TOILET PAPER!!

Let me tell you how that happened. One year I had a last-minute donation from a church for the Gift Bags. We had already filled the bags, tied them up with a bow, and they were ready to be handed out. I didn't know what to do with the extra money and asked the Inmate Chapel Clerks what we could get that would be really appreciated. One inmate said: "Chap, how about some soft toilet paper?" the other Clerks' eyes lit up and said, "Yes, yes, yes." Our DOC toilet paper is pretty rough to put it mildly. So, I went to the Warden's office to ask if this was ok. He looked at me funny, after I explained what I wanted to buy—800 rolls of soft toilet paper. He thought for a minute, then said, "I guess it's OK, Chaplain, but I don't quite understand it." Well, he wouldn't—he's a guy. The women love it.

We call the inmates down by dorm and they go through a cheerfully decorated line in the Chapel Auditorium and pick up their gift bag items as they go through the line. We have an inmate roster list, and we check them off the list as they come in. Not that they would try to come through the line *twice*, but it sometimes happens.

We play touching, nostalgic Christmas songs like: "Rock Around the Christmas Tree", "Jingle Bells", etc.

We keep what's in the gift bags pretty generic and called Holiday Gift Bags so ALL inmates will be welcome to come to the Chapel and get a Gift Bag.

I also try to visit SHU, that is made up of cells. Inmates who do not behave are put here for a specified time. At Christmas time, I usually wear my reindeer ears. I didn't ask anyone if I could do this – I just did it. One Christmas, I walked into SHU with my reindeer antlers on and all the inmates in the cells just laughed and then started crying. I announced for all to hear that Santa and I already knew they were on the "Naughty List "or they wouldn't be in SHU. I showed them their Holiday Gift Bags. Because it's SHU, they couldn't have them, but the bags were put in their property space to receive when they get out of SHU.

I was in SHU one Christmas, and I didn't realize that our Chief of Security was showing a newly hired officer around the compound and SHU. I heard him whisper to the Chief, who is that with the reindeer ears on? Chief smiled weakly and said: "That's our Chaplain."

An inmate once told me with tears in her eyes after receiving her Gift Bag that she could not believe she actually got a Gift Bag, music and laughter and love during Christmas. She said she had the best Christmas she had ever had in her life—and it was in PRISON. She said she really didn't have a family at all, and later told me that she cried, and laughed all the way back to her dorm.

Although it doesn't immediately solve everything, *love* and *kindness* are powerful forces when you have hardly experienced either one.

There is a nationwide organization called "Prison Fellowship." Prison Fellowship has structured, concentrated Bible Studies which are taught in most prisons, and they bless inmates' kids at Christmas in every prison facility in the United States: It is called "Angel Tree Program"; not to be confused with Salvation Army's Angel Tree. Here is how it works:

1. The inmate fills out a form to participate and they can choose from a great list of gifts they think their kids would like.

2. Chaplain turns them in to the Prison Fellowship organization.

3. The organization separates the applications by zip code.

4. Churches in the area where the kids are call the caregivers of the children first to see if they want the kids to receive the presents.

5. Churches buy the items and deliver the Christmas presents to the kids OR they sometimes have a Christmas party for the kids at the church where they hand out the presents that are tagged "From Mom" or "From Dad". This gives kids lots of peace and joy while their mom's and/or Dads are in prison. This is an excellent outreach for the respective Churches. Sometimes the church also hands out a sack of

groceries and if there are any older kids in the home, they minister to them also. It's a win-win program.

I love, admire, and respect Prison Fellowship. They do so much nationwide for inmates and their children. They hold special yard-wide revivals, called Hope Events, have correspondence Bible Studies for inmates and for their children. They have a special course for Wardens and have people presenting a solid curriculum, taught year-round to renew minds, give encouragement and hope to incarcerated men and women.

I am so thankful for them.

CHAPTER 19

Reentry

Reentry is a critical time, especially in the first six months. It's only a time when inmates are out but a time that will determine whether they will come back to prison or "make it." We tell inmates so much before they leave things that are much easier said than done. We say:

- Get a job
- Don't go back to your families if they are on drugs
- Stay away from all your "friends" who still do drugs
- Pay all the fines you owe (sometimes they owe thousands of dollars in court fines)
- Find a safe place to live
- Continue to attend Celebrate Recovery, AA/NA or other programs

We many classes that range from facility issues to helping offenders find places to go when they get out of prison. This is one of the factors that factor into whether inmates make it and stay out of prison, or if they mess up and must return. Reentry is an integral part of their rehabilitation. Women need to have a safe place to go to when released from prison. There are many, but not enough "transition houses" that women getting out of prison can go to. These are not connected to the Department of Corrections. Rather, they are run by people who know the need, and are willing to meet that need.

All of the transition houses I know of are faith-based. They will require that an inmate they are helping go to the church that supports that particular transition house. It is faith-based people who finance and support these vital transition houses.

Even the most cynical prison staff members do not agree with the inmates getting out and being responsible for paying literally hundreds or thousands of dollars' worth of fines from different counties. Staff and I agree that serving their time in prison should be the punishment. The fines should be dropped, and prison is their "payback" to society.

We know when inmates get out, they are trying to find a job, get their life together and are blessed if they can even get a minimum-wage job. They have no way of paying their fines; they are overwhelmed.

Upon release, an inmate gets $50 and a bus ticket to wherever in the state they want to go. They may have some money in their account they may have accumulated during the time they were incarcerated, but usually it's not much. A certain percentage of their "monthly salary" ($10-$25) goes into their personal account to be returned to them when they leave.

This is a very challenging and scary time for women getting out of prison. We are basically telling them to change their entire lives and do everything right.

Volunteers to the Rescue

Reentry is another whole dimension of rehabilitation – and a very necessary one.

For inmates, when they are in prison, this is a time when they pray to God: Get me out of here, get me out of here. Then, as it comes closer to their release, it's more like: Oh, my gosh, I'm getting out of here, and I'm scared— YIKES!"

First, when inmates get out of prison, they may feel that they are "fixed." After all, they are off drugs, they have taken classes, they have learned some life lessons, etc. However, we as Christians realize we are never really "fixed." We need God the Father, God the Son and God the Holy Spirit to help us through *all* the days of our lives.

A *literal* lifesaver is what we call a transition house. It's an actual house that houses and helps women during that transition time which is so crucial to a successful life on the outside.   Although not connected to the Department of Corrections, case managers and Chaplains work closely with transitions houses to ensure our women have a place to go when they get out.

Transition houses are usually a two, three, or four-bedroom house where ex-inmates go to live until they can get everything, they need to make it. We encourage inmates to apply within about three months of their discharge date to go live in one of these houses, where they will have a safe place to go and live anywhere from six months to a year. Every transition house has rules.

The ex-inmates must find a job (with the transition house's administrator's help). It's not easy for someone fresh out of prison to just go to a job interview and say they just got out of prison *yesterday* and they need a job. But the people running the transition houses help anyone staying in their transition house find a job – usually with people who know the person just got out of prison and are willing to try to help.

Transition houses require that they find a job, but keep the house clean, go to church at least twice a week, and *do not* have a "relationship" with anyone until they have been at the transition house for about a year. They are required to get along with other women in the house, who are also trying to work life. Usually, they will require ongoing attendance at the nearest "Celebrate Recovery" class.

> **"To make it your ambition and definitely endeavor to live quietly and peacefully, to mind your own affairs, and to work with your hands, as we charged you. So that you may bear**

yourselves becomingly and be correct and honorable and command the respect of the outside world, being dependent on nobody, self-supporting, and having need of nothing."
I Thessalonians 4:11,12 (AMP)

Sometimes an inmate will say she doesn't want to move to a transition house. I always ask, "Why not?" I know what they are going to say, I've heard it enough. They say they are getting prison and are "tired of 'rules' and don't want to go there and be told what to do."

I tell them frankly: Welcome to life. Life has rules. *I* have rules. When I close the gate behind me when I come to work every day, I am told what I need to do, what I can wear and not wear, what time I must go to lunch, what time I must get back from lunch, what time I need to report to work and what I am expected to do—report deadlines included.

"For the commandment is a lamp and, the whole teaching of the law is light, and reproofs of discipline are the way of life."
Proverbs 6:23 (AMP)

"For truth is a bright beam of light shining into every area of your life, instructing and correcting you to discover the ways to godly living."
Proverbs 6:23 (TPT)

Transition Houses *really* make a difference. After a woman has lived at the transition house for about a year, she can go look for a better job and honestly say, "Yes, I was in prison, but for the last year I have worked at ...wherever... and I have a letter of recommendation from my previous employer." This works!

Most of the women I know who have successfully transitioned from prison life to real life have lived in a transition house to help them get started. Remember: almost all of the women have fines to pay, and they really need help, and many have families that, quite frankly, are not good for the woman to be around.

How would you like to get out of prison and leave all family and friends, and even your kids for a while, take a minimum-wage job while trying to live a kind of life you have never lived before? Oh, by the way—you also owe $30,000 in court fines from when you were out there running crazy.

Ironically, (and wonderfully), most transition houses are run by ex-inmates themselves, who have successfully transitioned, and they *really* want to help women start over, after they are released from prison. They know how hard it is and they reach out. And they also know all the manipulative games woman may try to use to get around doing what she needs to do.

They don't "play." They tell them, one infraction of the rules of the house and you will be kicked out and on your own. Sound harsh? Well, there are about 40 women waiting for the empty bed—so if they don't want to follow rules, here's what they say: NEXT!

They are not trying to be harsh, but if a woman leaves the transition house, that is trying to help her, she will probably go back to drugs.

Once an inmate brought her discharge papers to me to sign. She informed me she was leaving in about an hour. Usually, we have more time than that, but sometimes not. I told her I was concerned about her because I had not helped her find a transition house. She replied that she had a place to go. I said, "Back to Mr. Yum-Yum?" She said, "Well, chaplain, I'm going to the guy's house who used to be my Mr. Yum-Yum. But we don't have that kind of relationship anymore. He said I could stay at his house. I told her that might not work, and she needed a fresh start. She said, "Well, chap, I think it will work—unless his wife gets jealous."

I say this frequently to women who are close to getting out: Not one woman who goes out that prison gate thinks she is ever coming back here – but unfortunately, they do. Sometimes four or five times. Usually, it's because they don't want to be told what to do, they want to be free. However, their idea of "freedom" sometimes is their downfall. Prison is a controlled environment. The transition houses are somewhat controlled, but life isn't.

> **"For you, brethren, were indeed called to freedom; only do not let your freedom be an incentive to your flesh..."**
> **Galatians 5:13 (AMP)**

Let me describe some instances of the struggle with reentry.

One of my chapel clerks was in her 50's. When she got out, she found a job in a restaurant. She was thankful for the job. She lived about three miles from work. She had no car. Some women would have just said "forget it," it's too far to walk.

This determined, wonderful lady walked the three miles to work and three miles home from work – for a year. She made pretty good money there and really liked working there. Now this lady was smart enough and skilled enough to work in an office, but she enjoyed the restaurant job. She still had court fines from before her incarceration to pay and living expenses.

The second year she purchased a bicycle and rode it to work.

The third year she purchased a "clunker" car, but she was grateful she didn't have to walk or ride her bike during the rain or winter.

The fourth year, she was able to afford an almost new car and was so proud of herself. She had a right to be proud and I was proud of her, too.

Another wonderful lady who got out of Eddie Warrior had fines all over the state of Oklahoma, thousands of dollars of them. She *had* to have a job. She finally found a job at a nice hotel in the Tulsa area. The thing was the guy who hired her knew she *had* to have a job. He made her a deal. She would give her word to work for him for at least two years. During those two years, she would work as many hours as he needed *and* he would *only* pay her minimum wage for each hour – no matter how many hours she worked. During the next two years, she averaged 60 hours per week; sometimes working six or seven days a week.

Others were telling her to quit, but she said she knew she was being taken advantage of because she was an ex-felon, but that she had given her word that she would comply. It was a *long* two years for her—but she kept her word.

At the end of two years, she applied many places but was turned down. Finally, she tried to go through a temp agency, thinking they might be able to open doors for her. She knew she had the attitude and aptitude to do a good job—she just couldn't seem to catch a break. The temp agency tested her skills, and they were sure they could find her a good job—until they found out she was an ex-felon. They informed her that their contracts with potential employees stated they would *not* send anyone to them on an assignment that had a record.

She was really getting discouraged by this time. But the temp agency called her not long after her interview to tell her they could not send her out, but they could hire her to work in the agency! They loved her. Not long after she started working for the temp agency, she helped another ex-felon friend of hers get a job at the temp agency. The agency loved her, too. These two women are two of the most steadfast women of integrity I ever met in prison—and believe me, I have met a lot of women of integrity who spent time at EWCC.

When they were at EWCC, they were each involved with Christian Women's Association, and they attended Victory Bible College. They were leaders in the Christian community at Eddie Warrior.

They both worked with this temp agency for two years. They left the agency only because each one of them got a job with a nation-wide prison ministry making a lot more money and doing something that was more than a job—it was a "calling"—to help women and men still incarcerated salvage their lives. I still keep in touch with them after several years they have been out of prison. I am so glad they are successful.

One of the main goals of my chaplaincy was reentry, which was not recognized for several years after I started. Volunteers and staff were not permitted to have any kind of contact with an ex-inmate for the first six months they are out of prison. Oops! And that's their most vulnerable time and the time when most fail—a time when they *really* need help.

In my role as chaplain, I was thinking about the reentry part of the lives of inmates. I didn't know exactly how to strengthen it. A volunteer who had been bringing in a monthly church service called me. He said that while church services were very important, God had dealt with him about helping inmates *after* they get out of prison. He began to network with other churches, volunteers *and* employers statewide. His program went statewide, and it started at EWCC. I worked with him and even told him he should establish as a non-profit, write his Mission Statement and *go for it.* I helped him, but the blessings of God were on this program.

This volunteer had a very lucrative business; he made a lot of money. But he gave it all up to help ex-inmates after they are released from prison. Life-changing is tough, but with God—definitely attainable. Reward for his sacrifice—the work itself: PLEASING GOD!

Another ex-inmate, now a badged volunteer, followed a vision she had of Jesus while she was incarcerated, of opening transition houses for women getting out of prison. She didn't open one successful, structured transition house – she currently has several houses. She has accomplished something in the natural that the Holy Spirit placed in her heart while she was in prison. God has richly blessed her as she has blessed others. She puts in over 60 hours per week; she is always on call. She doesn't put up with nonsense from an ex-inmate who is only playing games and doesn't really want to do what is necessary to change their life. After all, she *knows* those games. But her compassion and drive to help women coming out of prison supports and sustains her. She has saved many lives. She is an effective voice for prison reform for incarcerated women.

Many ex-offenders work with reentry. They know how *crucial* it is.

Another badged volunteer who was once incarcerated at EWCC, established a cosmetology school in a higher security level prison and is working to bring another cosmetology school to EWCC. She initially had the vision for this when she was at EWCC. When an inmate finishes her training, she is licensed. The wonderful, compassionate, capable lady is a Master Instructor of Cosmetology. Her vision is to give women a skill so they can make a living as they venture out to a new beginning. God gave her the vision to accomplish this while she was incarcerated at EWCC.

All of these volunteers really become a part of the women's lives to whom they minister. Remember: we are telling women coming out of prison to leave their families most of the time *and* their friends and make a new life. They need someone to be "connected to" that resembles, however limited, a family.

Just plain loneliness is something every woman getting out of prison has to deal with. I tell them that there *will* be times of loneliness, but if they follow God closely, He will fill that void.

> **"God places the solitary in families and gives the desolate a home in which to dwell; He leads the prisoners out to prosperity; but the rebellious dwell in a parched land."**
> **Psalms 68:6 (AMP)**

Interesting to note that all of these reentry programs are faith based. They are supported by churches. Participants are required to attend church. Church attendance is important for *anyone*, but especially for ex-inmates to be in *church*.

> **"Planted in the House of the Lord, they shall flourish in the courts of our God."**
> **Psalms 92:13 (AMP)**

After women get out of prison at EWCC, they usually join Facebook and stay in touch. Social media helps them stay accountable and less isolated.

One woman, who was incarcerated at EWCC, had decided that rather than go to a transition house when she got out, she wanted to go live with her mom. She assured me her mom was not on drugs or anything like that. I really felt led to advise her to go to a transition house first, then after a time she could go to live with her mom if she still wanted to. She went to her mom's house. About six months after she left, she called me to say said she was not doing well. Her mom was fine, but she was so isolated.

She said the town was so small, that there were no jobs. She didn't have a car, so she couldn't get a job far away and she had forgotten how negative her mom could be. She wasn't criticizing her mom. A lot of inmates go to "take care" of their moms when they get out: they feel obligated. But she said she felt herself "slipping."

Returning home usually just doesn't work, because women need to build a life of their own and then reach out to their families to help them, if they can. I located a transition house that would take her. Usually, transitions houses don't take anyone who has been out for a while. They only take women who come straight out of prison. No, they can't stop by and visit with Mr. Yum-Yum.

An inmate who had gotten out of prison about six months earlier called me. After the initial "How are you?" pleasantries, she said, "Chap, I'm doing pretty good, got a job, etc. I don't have any desire for drugs or alcohol but Mr. Yum-Yum is starting to look really good! Help me!" We both started laughing. She knew what I was going to say about that: 'No Mr. Yum-Yum until you have been out at least a year –probably longer.' She laughed again and said, "Thanks, Chap. I just needed a little pep talk. I'm getting back on track."

Reentry has blossomed in the Oklahoma Department of Corrections over the last 18 years. I'm so glad that it has and that woman who were at EWCC have become a part of the solution—and are no longer a part of the problem.

CHAPTER 20

The Inmates

When I share about inmates, I do not use any names to protect the innocent *and* the *guilty.* But truthfully, it's because I'm afraid I will leave some lady's name out and I have been blessed with *so many* great inmates Chapel workers and volunteers over the years, that I don't want to leave any of them out! They have truly been a blessing to me and to the Chapel programs.

How did I change from being totally unsympathetic towards women who have broken the law to being genuinely compassionate towards women who were incarcerated?

I MET THEM.

As I said, I went into Prison to find "inmates" – but instead, I found WOMEN: broken Women, desperate Women, weary Women, emotionally-worn Women.

> **"The Lord is close to those who are of a broken heart and saves such as are crushed with sorrow for sin and humbly and thoroughly penitent."**
> **Psalms 34:18 (AMP)**

At times, I have gotten frustrated with them, but *so* many *more* times I have admired them, convinced that I don't really know how they have done as much as they have simply surviving, considering where many of them came from. I really don't know if I could have done as well.

Female inmates are individuals. Sometimes when we talk about "inmates" in a general way, we don't mean to lump them all in one bag, leaving the impression that they are all alike—they are not! However, they do have some basic attitudes that are common to most inmates.

I always have a small percentage of female inmates who will tell me: "Chaplain, I was raised right; this was not my parent's fault. I became disobedient, got with the wrong crowd; started doing drugs; and then drugs started doing me."

But, so much more often they come from horrible backgrounds. Their view of life is distorted, and their hearts are broken. They had lots of people around them, but no one to protect them.

Most women incarcerated started doing strong drugs at a *very* young age. The "high" deadens a pain they cannot explain.

Sometimes, I have left after a busy day and on my way home, I've thanked God for allowing me to really help some lady, in particular. Other times, I have told God I'm thankful that he can unscramble eggs—because I can't. The women's' lives seem to be *such* a mess. I just don't have all the answers. But God does.

Eddie Warrior, as well as other prisons in the state has some people who would be better helped if they were sent to a mental hospital. But we don't have those facilities in Oklahoma anymore. So, they end up coming to prison.

One inmate came to me and said, "Chaplain, I'm getting out soon and I don't know if I should go back to my first child's dad or the second child's dad or the third child's dad or back to my old boyfriend because he is getting out of prison soon, too." I replied, "How about *none* of the above?

How about going to a transition house and getting a job and getting a little help and *then* make that decision?"

None of the women incarcerated want to be in prison, but they admit that it's the best thing that could have happened to them. It's practically impossible to just wake up one morning with Mr. Yum-Yum in your bed and say: "I'm kicking his druggy self out and I'm going to rehab, and I'm going to get a good job and take care of my children, etc., etc., etc." When they come to prison, however, they are off the "merry-go-round" of the life they were living, and they have a chance for that "new beginning" that God speaks of in His Word.

> **"Look, I am about to do something new; even now it is coming. Do you not see it? Indeed, I will make a way in the wilderness, rivers in the desert."**
> **Isaiah 43:19**

So, I believe in prison. However, the sentences in Oklahoma are way too long for women. In the first place, we have more women incarcerated per capita than any other state. And the sentences are *so long* for women. So long that their kids are grown, and their family members have passed away and their *hope* for a new beginning seems too far away to do anything about it. Women get longer sentences than men for the same crime. Are all the sentences fair? No, but the Department of Corrections has nothing to say about the sentencing of *any* inmate. That decision is made *before* they get to prison.

The Department of Corrections is NOT the enemy: SIN IS. It actually started with the sin of the person who molested them.

There was, however, one personality trait that I struggled with and repented over for years. I was never really much of a crier (unless, of course if I wanted to manipulate my husband with tears.) In my heart I had genuine empathy for struggling people, and would pray for them and counsel them, but I just hardly ever cried. I felt that maybe my heart was not concerned for others. Yet this character trait turned out to be one of my greatest assets as a Chaplain. I heard about horrible, heart-wrenching situations and had to break the news of a death of an inmate's family member on a regular basis. I had to be strong and steady *every day* as a Chaplain.

I do know this: what God has done in the lives of women here at EWCC is truly miraculous and amazing.

I have always tried to be a good example to follow instructions and obey rules and guidelines, especially concerning my relationships and dealings with inmates. However, I have to say that I broke one guideline consistently. As staff, we are not supposed to tease or laugh it up with inmates. Our relationship with them *has* to be professional. I agree with being professional: no off-color jokes; sexual remarks; and no gossiping about other staff, etc., but the guideline I did break was laughing with the inmates.

I have to confess we (me and EWCC inmates) laughed *every* day: sometimes *every hour* of the day. Or when teaching classes, we laughed. I like to tease anyway, but they needed to laugh as they are healed and strengthened by this new-found freedom planted in their hearts and spirits.

Humor and joy have always been a part of me. Laughter is good like a medicine. I have always been a kidder and I have always LOVED to laugh! I was strict as far as inmate behavior was concerned, but I was also quick to laugh.

> "It was like a dream come true when you freed us from our bondage and brought us back to Zion. We laughed and laughed and overflowed with gladness. We left shouting for joy and singing your praise. All the nations saw it and joined in, saying, "The Lord has done great miracles for them!" Yes, He did mighty miracles, and we are overjoyed! Now Lord, do it again! Restore us to our former glory! May streams of your refreshing flow over us until our dry hearts are drenched again. Those who sow their tears as seeds will reap a harvest with joyful shouts of glee. They may weep as they go out carrying their seed to sow, but they will return with joyful laughter and shouting with gladness as they bring back armloads of blessing and a harvest overflowing."
> **Psalms 126 (TPT)**

The thing we laughed at the most was *ourselves*.

Glitches in My Radar

I don't know about everyone else, but I do know when I was first saved, I was *really* dedicated to God, but I still had a few "glitches in my radar."

197

Here's an example of my phrase. Not long after my husband and I were saved, I was a happy new Christian, but then my husband told me that we were going to start tithing. What? No! I told him if you start tithing, I'm going to leave you! I had two kids and one on the way *soon*! I loaded them up in the car and drove off—for about an hour. Then I came back. Where the heck was I going to go? We got it all straightened out and we've been tithing ever since. (Radar Glitch)

One male inmate, who was a really *big* guy, had been incarcerated for years before he got saved in prison. Feared by many, he was sent from prison to prison. He was in maximum-security prison most of the time; he was really tough! But he got saved and dedicated his life to God. Many guys were still afraid of him, but he started going to church and started doing the right thing. He was a happy new Christian.

Then he started inviting other inmates to the church services he was attending in prison. Other inmates, still afraid of this big guy, would say "Yes" they would attend that night's services. *But* what if they didn't show up? He would find them and beat them. He said that one night, as he was beating up a fellow inmate, he heard a voice say, "What are you doing?" He said, "I'm beating them up for you, Jesus." They said they were coming to church, but they didn't." The voice said to him: "Stop it." And he did. (Radar Glitch)

One female inmate at EWCC who was a happy new Christian, came to my office to tell me she and another inmate were very seriously going on a serious fast to seek God. I said that was great, but that she may want to only fast a thing or a meal and reminded her that she still had to work every day. All inmates have some kind of a job. I told her that would be a challenge if she fasted *everything*. She said that it was going to be okay because she had stolen a few apples from Food Service, so they could eat that during their serious fast. We laughed about it later. (Radar Glitch)

Another female inmate wanted me to read the letter she had written to the Parole Board to see what I thought. Often, inmates would ask me to read their letter to the Parole Board to give them suggestions on the tone of the letter. I advise inmates not to talk too much about their religious conversion experience. It's fine to mention it, but don't write a sermon. Judges and Parole Boards have heard that enough. Instead, I encourage them to list all the classes they have taken (faith-based and non-faith based), and *all* they have accomplished education-wise. She left me to read her letter.

When she returned, I told her that more than three or four times she made references such as: "I'm on fire for God", "I have a "burning fire in my soul to get back with my kids", "I will not put out the flame in my heart", and a few other statements about being "on fire." Knowing the answer already, I asked her what her charge was? She re-read her letter—thought for a minute, and then said "Oh, my gosh, Chaplain, you know it was arson?! Then she burst out laughing. I have way too many references to 'fire' right, Chaplain?" (Radar Glitch) We laughed and laughed and then laughed some more.

Another female inmate came by to introduce herself to me when she arrived from higher security prison (Mabel Basset) to EWCC. My heart broke for her. She was rough looking. Because of the severity of the lives they have lived, a lot of inmates look about 10 years older than they really are. Life, in general, has not been good to them. She seemed timid but determined. She informed me that she had gotten saved recently. I welcomed her. We talked for a minute, and then I didn't see her for a few weeks. I wanted to talk to her again, but I had forgotten her name so I couldn't page her to come to my office. We have so much going on, so many inmates (800-900) at any given time and an average sentence of three years, it was sometimes hard to keep up with every inmate who visited my office. I always tried to stop and talk to them, even if it was just for a few minutes because I was so busy.

Sometimes they just need someone to listen.

Then one morning, she came to my office. I thanked God under my breath for sending her to me to give me a second chance to talk with her. She had tears in her eyes and seemed kind of confused. I asked her how she was doing? She said, "Chaplain, I think God said something to me this morning when I woke up—do you think it was really God?"

"Well, what did you hear?"

She stared down at the floor. "You know, chap, I've worked the streets and done a lot of" ...her voice trailed off... but she went on to say, "I heard a voice say, 'You are holy and pure unto Me.' Do you think that could have been God saying that to me?"

This was one of the few times I was brought to tears. I took her hand. She lifted her chin and looked at me fully in the face. I said, "Yes, without a doubt, that was God. Don't ever forget that, because when He looks at you, he sees you as holy and pure no matter what your past." "Really?" she asked. "Yes," I said, "Really."

> **"To open their eyes that they may turn from darkness to light and from the power of Satan to God, so that they may thus receive forgiveness and release from their sins and a place and portion among those who are consecrated and purified by faith in Me."**
> **Acts 26:18 (AMP)**

Chapel Clerks

My desk was a mess, and I was always losing stuff like files, reports, important papers. But the inmate Chapel Clerks would ask me if I had looked in my "monster drawer" for what I needed. I had one drawer that was almost as messy as the top of my desk. I would usually find it. If they would think of some really brilliant strategy as far as the

Chapel was concerned, I would just tell them I would take the credit for the idea—and they needed to get back to work!

I got valuable input from the chapel clerks. They knew how things *really* worked on the dorms—and what *wasn't* working well as far as the chapel programs were concerned. I would thank them for their input which we would consider. I tried to give them as much space to grow and expand their perspectives. I gave them as much responsibility as I could without jeopardizing Security.

It was kind of a privilege on the yard to work in the chapel. Inmates had to apply for a job in the chapel just like other jobs on the yard, except that they had to be Level 4 inmates and they had to exhibit good behavior. I didn't want any inmate who had just been informed about a death or emergency in her family to have to hear someone who worked in the chapel use the "F" word or be cussing and screaming. Character and behavior were required to be a chapel clerk. This is the group that I attempted to "mentor" and this was only possible because I worked with them every day.

I couldn't really mentor 800 women. I could get volunteers to get the Gospel to them and make classes available to them, but the volunteer chaplains and I could really "impart" into the lives of these chapel clerks. And they worked hard. We always had a lot going on in the chapel. Many times, if I worked through lunch, they (voluntarily) worked through lunch. If I worked late, they (voluntarily) worked late.

One inmate came to me to apply for a job as a chapel "Orderly," the job of the orderly was to clean the whole chapel. I asked her if she would mind cleaning our bathrooms? This question also revealed their real attitude about the job. If they seemed hesitant about cleaning bathrooms, I wouldn't hire them. But this particular inmate said, "No, chaplain, my mom never taught me how to do *any* housework, but if you will have someone show me *how* to clean a bathroom, the water Baptismal and the whole chapel, I guarantee I will be the best and hardest chapel worker you've ever had." And she was. She was also quick to tell me, while she didn't have any cleaning skills, "I could get the needle, fill the syringe and shoot my mom up on her drugs by the age of eight." She might have missed a thing or two once in a while, but her attitude was always positive.

One inmate came to my office, and we had a conversation about her mom and grandmother. She said they came to her when she was about 15 years old and told her that she was old enough to get a job and they needed her to do so. She asked: What kind of job? They told her to do the same job they were doing: stripping in clubs. So, she did.

Female inmates are allowed to wear some makeup. They are allowed a base, lipstick and mascara. I don't know who determined this, but whoever it was certainly has my vote. Color us "carnal", but it does help our self-esteem to feel that we *look good*. But they have to buy it through our "Canteen", it can't be sent from home. And who doesn't look better with makeup? Makeup ranks right up there with soft toilet paper for us!!

One inmate came to me and said when she called home her husband was not receiving what she had to say about the Gospel, now that she was saved. In one way, it is endearing that they want to save their whole family now that they have accepted Jesus into their hearts.. However, it doesn't carry much weight when you tell your family what *they* need to do now that you know everything spiritual--God and I are so spiritual. Let them see you walk it out after you get out—that's what they are waiting to see.

One inmate's mother called me to say that I might want to keep an eye on her daughter who was incarcerated at EWCC. She was going to have to tell her that she was adopting her two very young grandchildren and was going to file a motion to *never* let her daughter see her children again. She was also filing a restraining order, in case she tried to come home to see them. The mother started crying at this point. She said, "Chaplain, I am a Christian and I love my daughter, but this is her third time in prison. She seems to do well while she is incarcerated, and during that time her calls home consist of telling her two little girls about how she has changed, and how much she misses them and will pick them up the minute she gets out—which she has done two times. [And] both times she has gotten out, picked her two little girls up [from] out of my house, hooked up with some guy from the street or one she used to do drugs with and starts doing drugs again.

And, Chaplain, *each time*, my two little granddaughters were sexually molested by more than one guy. They come to me broken and confused. I get them into counseling, settle them down with lots of love and structure and security, and then this happens again. I have had these two sweet babies of mine in extensive counseling and about the time they are starting to get better, my daughter gets out of prison and does the *same thing* each time. I had to make a decision—it's really a choice: my daughter or my granddaughters. I love my daughter, but she is an adult. But for the mental and emotional survival of my granddaughters, I have to keep her away from them. They need healing time and stability in their life to get well." I told her I was *so* sorry about her situation. Families are really put through a lot.

Most families of inmates *try* to be supportive, but quite honestly, when the woman finally gets to prison, family is just plain old "worn out." It's tough on them, too.

Another family member spoke to me during a visiting day. She told me her daughter, who is in prison, thinks she's mean because when she calls home to tell her how hard it is in prison, she says, "Well, I'm serving *your* prison time as much as you are." She went on to tell me how her daughter's incarceration had affected her life. She said, "Chaplain, I'm a widow and in my late 60's. I met a widower in his early 70's. We grew very fond of each other and were blessed that we both wanted to "travel" as we grew even older. We married and traveled in our small camper and were really enjoying our relationship. You know, Chaplain, relationships are a little different when you are older. What you want to do in your remaining years means a lot to you.

Anyway, then my daughter went to prison and my life changed drastically. She had three children under the age of five. If I didn't get custody of them, I might never have seen them again. So, I got custody and started raising these three little ones. No more traveling for us. My husband was good to try to help me with them, but after about a year of raising the kids, he came to me declaring how much he admired me for raising my three grandchildren and said that he might have done the same thing. He also said he would help me financially, but that he no longer wanted to be married. He stated that he was now in his mid-70's and just staying home and raising three little kids is not the way he wanted to live out his last years. Some may say he was selfish, but honestly, I totally understood. He helps me a little financially, but we are no longer married. So, Chaplain, I don't have a whole lot of sympathy for my daughter when she tells me how unhappy she is in prison. I *love* my grandchildren, but I sometimes selfishly feel that I am in a bit of a prison – a love prison - but still a prison."

When you help a woman in prison, you are helping her children, her family, and her community.

Following are more "testimonies" of women who were incarcerated at EWCC but have gone on to prove themselves over the years that they have been out of prison. I'll let them open their stories and their hearts to you.

Loving Women Back to Life

TAMMY

I was raised in a dysfunctional family full of poverty, filth and neglect, I began using drugs at the age of 13. Many nights, the only light in my childhood home was the glow of the living room TV. I would find my father drunk, if he were there at all. My mom would be asleep on the couch. It was a dark, filthy place. For years, I struggled with the lies that I had been fed: that I was worthless, no good, a mistake. The trauma and abuse I lived with led to a life of bad choices and addiction. At 13 years old, I ran away from home to search for the love I craved. I had a baby girl at age 14 and gave the child up for adoption. By the time I was 15, I was shooting meth intravenously.

Once, I was beaten and left for dead by a stranger. I look at my teenage granddaughter now. I realize that I was only a child, but for all those years, I just thought I was a *really bad* person. I ended up spending 18 years of my adult life in prison. I didn't believe I was capable of change. I was caught up in a very, very dark world. And I couldn't for the life of me, find the way out. I couldn't find the door.

Broken and full of shame, I wanted to give up when I was sent back to prison the fourth time, at the age of 50, with a brand new 20-year sentence. I carried that shame into Eddie Warrior Correctional Center for what would be my *final* prison stint.

On that big prison yard, there was a chapel led by Chaplain Kathryn McCollum. Chaplain had *knit together* a program that allowed volunteers of *all* faiths, denominations and backgrounds to come in and provide services and programs for the women who were incarcerated there.

I was desperate, exhausted, and at the end of my rope. When I saw the steeple on the chapel as the van drove me into the EWCC yard, it literally called out to me in a way that I cannot find the words to express. It wasn't long after I had been placed inside the fence that I found myself going through the front door of the chapel. I will never forget how I walked in with my head held down so far in shame. I had been at this facility before, and I knew the Chaplain would recognize me.

I was so embarrassed and fully expecting her to condemn me for being back at a place I should have never returned to. But it was just the opposite. The Chaplain looked at me with compassion and love and in our first conversation she said, "You want a job?" I was blown away. No judgment, no condemnation, but a chance to get it right this time. I accepted her offer and became one of the chapel clerks: a *very* coveted job at EWCC.

Being introduced to Christ as a child, I dug deep into the Christian-led programs that were offered. The volunteers who came to lead us would look us in the eye and speak to us like we *mattered*. They taught the Bible, saying there was a better way than how we had been living. They

211

led with kindness and love. When they said they would be there, they were true to their word.

I couldn't get it. Why would these people come and take their time out for me, and other women like me? I didn't understand that. I was in awe of the respect and honor I was shown by the chaplain and all the volunteers. They treated us like we were valuable and, the funny thing with that, is that the more people treat you that way, the easier it is for you to believe it yourself.

I began to watch *every* move the volunteers would make. I listened to every word they spoke. I knew they knew more than I did because they carried the keys to the chapel in their hand. I let that be a symbol for me. If you had keys and were able to walk out of prison at the end of the day, you were somebody I could learn from. Then I began to realize how much I wanted to be like them. I wanted to be the kind of person that spent her time caring for others more than I cared for myself.

After several years of serving in this chapel under Chaplain McCollum's leadership, I was finally released from prison. There is a scripture in the Bible that says God will use all things for our good and His Glory IF we allow Him to. This promise has proven to be so true in my life since I surrendered my life to Him and learned who I was through this chapel program at EWCC.

Today, I have my own set of keys. I am a program manager for Prison Fellowship Academy at Mabel Bassett correctional Center, where I check in each morning and leave every evening. I have keys to my office and to the classroom at the prison where I have the honor of leading women in this program and showing them the same respect and love that was shown to me. It is so much more than I could have ever have asked or imagined. Every single day, I am so grateful for my time at EWCC Chapel, the place I learned my true identity in Christ and my worth.

Forty-seven felonies. Four incarcerations. ONE LIFE REDEEMED!

CHRISTIE

My name is Christie Luther. I am the Founder and Executive Director of the R.I.S.E. Program, Oklahoma's first Cosmetology school in a women's prison in Oklahoma.

Sent to Prison

I would like to share about discovering God's intentional redemption in my life in the most unlikely place; a place called prison. In 2008, I was sentenced to prison for five years because I caused a tragic accident that claimed the life of a man. I am not sure if someone can even begin to imagine the shame and guilt I felt because of my negligence, but the enemy used it daily to remind me of the hopelessness I felt.

As a child, I was *not* raised in church. I was abused in every way possible, which caused me to wander around living a broken existence while trying to maneuver life on my own terms. I came to know the Lord and embrace my salvation when I was 23 years old, but I had no mentors or encouragement, so I lived a *mediocre* Christian life, but did not know God fully until I arrived at EWCC.

While incarcerated, God began to heal me and do a transforming work in me. Although the transformation was painful, I knew I needed Him because I was convinced that He had a grandiose plan for me. Our Chaplain, Chaplain McCollum, became my mentor and teacher. The work that the Lord did in that place was largely because of her and I thank God for all that I learned there.

214

I was a graduate of the first class of Victory Bible College at EWCC, and I recall and miss the days when I could sit at Jesus' feet for 8-10 hours per day and learn. I worked in the Law Library and the Beauty Shop. I have been a licensed Cosmetologist for 33 years. It was while I was literally doing a shampoo in the prison beauty shop that I heard God speak to me and said, "I want you to start a cosmetology school in prison."

Well, while wearing 'INMATE' on the back of your shirt, it seemed improbable. But I know that God was faithful, and He would see this through. Now we fast forward eight years later, I have received a pardon from Governor Stott, and I am the Executive Director of a non-profit RISE Cosmetology School. I have a beautiful relationship with the Lord, friends, family, my students, and my daughters, who spent time on the playground at EWCC. I have been appointed by the Governor as a Board member for the Oklahoma Board of Cosmetology and Barbering. I could go on and on about the Presence and the favor of God in my life, but the truth is that I am just His vessel, His Hands and Feet.

I am honored to serve my God who revealed Himself to me while in prison. I could not have done any of this on my own. He made it happen. He opened the doors. He softened hearts as He healed my brokenness. I am honored to serve my God who revealed Himself to me while in prison. He calls me valuable and brought me inside the prisons—to teach, love, and bring hope to incarcerated women. I understand them because I have been there, and God used my time in prison as a megaphone to speak to them and bring them hope.

If He did it for me, He can bring redemption to all.

BETH

Eleven years ago, my life was changed forever! My husband of 15 years and I were arrested together for the nasty, criminal, and dangerous business of manufacturing methamphetamine. Our lives had been spared and on that day our journey back to life and light began.

We were caught in a death trap and had lost everything. Soon, we realized that it wouldn't have been long before our lives were gone, and we were being lowered down into our physical graves. However, we were already dead spiritually. We knew and had seen demons and called them by name. The darkness that consumed us had stolen everything good that was left in our world. I felt like the manufacturing charges were the least of what we had done against our family, ourselves, and against the community. I knew I deserved whatever consequences would be handed down and I felt fortunate that my charges were not worse.

I cried out to Jesus *with every fiber of my being* and hoped he was still listening to me. He was and He let me know that He *still* loved me!!

I served a 15-year sentence at EWCC, and the Lord blessed me daily by surrounding me with wonderful Godly women that led me and guided me into a new life. The wonderful women at the chapel offered my sisters and I hope—that we *could* have an amazing future and that we could live an abundant life on earth. We learned of forgiveness and that we were forgiven. I was allowed to sit at the feet of Jesus and graduated from Victory Bible College. I sat under Chaplain/Pastor McCollum, who truly loved me ad poured her heart into me. She walked me through the fire and held me accountable. I experienced every moment of the Lord refining me in that fire.

Only God could shine such light into a dark, hopeless place. When I look back to that time, the thousands of milestones and miracles along the way when Jesus was either holding me, carrying me, or leading me that have brought me to where I am today. I am so humbled!

Who are we that the God that created all of heaven and earth would see fit to save us and reform us rather than throw us away? After all we had done, everything bad against God that we could possibly think of! We were a pathetic example of His creation and we set out to damage His Kingdom as much as possible. We had become the worst of the worst! BUT it wasn't about who we were: it was about who HIS SON JESUS CHRIST was and that he died for our sins and they were already forgiven. It was made real that we were made righteous through HIM.

I'm so grateful today for the life I have, the family He has restored, and how he has replaced all that was lost. My husband and I have celebrated 22 years of marriage. He preaches now and ministers to the boys at Tulsa Boys Home.

I am blessed that we still have each other on the 11-year anniversary of our sobriety. We are blessed beyond measure that He would use us to help further His Kingdom for His glory!

Today, my husband and I own and operate a faith-based sober living home, His Open Door Ministry, Inc., that houses 20 ladies who have gotten out of prison. There isn't a single day that I don't see God bless our ladies in the same ways He did for us!

This year the Judge recognized the work we do and dismissed over $50,000 in fines for me! Praise God! His promises are true and His mercies are new every day! He had plans for us just like it is written in Jeremiah 29:11. He has prospered us! Lord, when I complain, please remind me who I am in You and that *You* are in control of my life and not me!! Without you, I am nothing!

In the midst of such madness and chaos in the world, thank you for being a God of peace that loves His people.

JOHNNA

After living a life addicted to meth, it finally caught up with me. In 2016, I was sentenced to 15 years in prison for possession of CDS (controlled dangerous substance) with intent to distribute. I knew who Jesus was but I was not living the Christian life living for HIM. Sitting in my jail cell talking to God I told him that whatever happens, I would follow Him. In January 2017, I made it to Eddie Warrior Correctional Center. I didn't know what to expect; I just knew that I needed to draw closer to Jesus and find myself. I became involved in as many Bible studies as were available and spent *a lot of time* at the chapel where I later became a clerk and a leader in a Reentry program.

Being denied a year review, I knew in my heart God had something better in store. On April 3, 2018, I received my daughter's graduation announcement with the words written on it "discharged to probation." I thought surely there was a mistake. Exactly three months to the day on July 4, 2018, a group of public defenders came in and wanted to take my case.

I continued to do the next right thing. God was showing me, and I was paying attention. On December 5, 2018, I made commutation, and the governor released me from prison to be reunited with my family. Since then, I have gotten my children back, my driver's license, bought my own car and many other positive things happened my life. I have recently been appointed director of "The Refuge." The Refuge is a women's transitional living house operated through Forgotten Ministries. I am living a life serving the Lord. I believe that is the least I could do for what He has done for me.

Those who have graduated chose a servant's role in life, as highlighted in the aforementioned testimonies of these four inmates. They describe where they came from and what they are doing now. Each one of them is in a ministry serving others today. It is amazing how many women who were incarcerated at Eddie Warrior ended up in full-time ministries because of what God spoke to them while they were incarcerated.

CHAPTER 21

Conclusion

"Not that we are fit, qualified and sufficient in ability of ourselves to form personal judgments or to claim or count anything as coming from us, but our power and ability and sufficiency are from God. It is He who has qualified us, making us to be fit and worthy and sufficient as ministers and dispensers of a new covenant of salvation through Christ, not ministers of the letter of legally written code, but of the Spirit; for the code of the Law kills, but the Holy Spirit makes alive."

II   Corinthians   3:5,6 (AMP)

I served at Eddie Warrior Correctional Center for 22 wonderful, challenging years for hundreds and hundreds of inmates whose sentences are an average of one to three years, and some much longer. Volunteer groups would consistently say they could sense the presence of God as they walked in to hold services on the yard.

I have the utmost respect for the Oklahoma Department of Corrections. They were good to me as an employee. They take care of thousands of Oklahoma inmates who basically hate them. Legislatures do not want to throw enough money the way of the Department of Corrections. So, DOC does the best *they* can to house, feed, teach, and generally help inmates.

Yet the inmates don't think so. The public doesn't think so. The volunteers may not think so. It's so easy to criticize what *you* don't *have* to do.

To repeat, DOC does NOT hand out sentences. DOC does NOT want more inmates. DOC is NOT the enemy— SIN IS.

Remember, I went into prison to find inmates. Instead, I found broken women, desperate women, weary women, and emotionally worn Women.

Not only did I grow to love all the many inmates who served as Chapel Workers and even those who didn't, and I respected and admired them because of what they had been through in their lives. Many were sweet little babies, born into abusive, ungodly, drug-infested homes where their innocence would be taken soon enough. They "modeled" what they saw and endured what they had absolutely no control over and didn't understand. And they accepted these circumstances as "normal."

The enemy gets a foothold in their lives and their development before they are even old enough to know what all that means. They grow up in a world of perversion, fear and confusion. No wonder they make lousy decisions. I am not making excuses for their actions, but there are root reasons for their poor choices.

> **"The strong spirit of a man sustains him in bodily pain or trouble, but a weak and broken spirit who can raise up or bear?"**
> **Proverbs 18:14 (AMP)**

> **"The will to live sustains you when you are sick, but depression crushes courage and leaves you unable to cope."**
> **Proverbs 18:14 (TPT)**

I believe in the power of MERCY and the power of TRUTH.

> **"Herald and preach the Word!**
> **Keep your sense of urgency stand by,**
> **be at hand and ready whether the**
> **opportunity seems to be favorable or**
> **unfavorable. Whether it is convenient**
> **or inconvenient, whether it is welcome**
> **or unwelcome, you as preacher of the**
> **Word are to show people in what way**
> **their lives are wrong. And convince**
> **them, rebuking and correcting,**
> **warning and urging and encouraging**
> **them, being unflagging and**
> **inexhaustible in patience and teaching."**
> **II Timothy 4:2 (AMP)**

I got a lot of praise and positive strokes from people when I was a Chaplain and I truly appreciate it, but…

> **"For who separates you from others?**
> **Who makes you superior and sets you**
> **apart from another, giving you the**
> **preeminence? What have you that was**
> **not given to you?...why do you boast as**
> **if you had not received it but had gained**
> **it by your own efforts?**
> **I Corinthians 4:7 (AMP)**

225

> **"Of this Gospel I was made a minister according to the gift of God's free Grace undeserved favor which was bestowed on me by the exercise, the working in all is effectiveness of His Power."**
>
> **Ephesians 3:7 (AMP)**

I got *a lot* of credit for what God and volunteers did for the women incarcerated at Eddie Warrior Correctional Center, a continual wave after wave of new inmates over the years.

To be honest, I was never really sure which inmates leaving EWCC were going to make it and which weren't. Some I thought surely would make it after they got out – didn't. Some I thought would NOT make it, did.

Let me point out that when I was truly called by God to Eddie Warrior, I was:

Almost 50 years old: a very late bloomer.

Not a "prayer warrior."

Some people say when they pray for what seems like five minutes, they look at the clock and see its has been an hour. I, on the other hand, pray for what seems like an hour, look up at the clock and find out it's been five minutes!

Not an avid studier or reader.

Ministers I know read three or four Christian books a month. I'm blessed to read one every three months.

Not as "spiritual" as a lot of Christians.

Not spending as much time in the Word (Bible) as I should.

The bottom line was that I was simply called and placed by God – *even* with all my faults. I don't have enough time to list all of those.

Work continually on your faults or shortcomings,
but don't let them get in the way of your gifts and callings.

A Pastor who helped with preaching at EWCC, and also worked with a prominent reentry group, told me before he left for a new out-of-state pastorate that he had been a Pastor for 10 years. He said that in the two years he had worked as a volunteer with us, he had never seen as many spiritually positive results as he had at EWCC.

I was called as a "WATERER." The apostle Paul wrote:

> **"I planted, Apollos watered, but God all the while was making it grow and He gave the increase. So neither he who plants is anything nor he who waters, but only God who makes it grow and become greater. He who plants and he who waters are equal."**
> **I Corinthians 3:6, 7, 8**
> **(AMP)**

Every program, service or class tripled, and quadrupled during that amazing 22 years.

You may be called to water and help nurture what someone else planted.

I was strict in some ways but tried always to be led by the Holy Spirit as to what a particular inmate who came to talk to me needed at the moment: a correction or just encouragement.

All the services, classes, counseling, donations, example-setting volunteers are responsible for the growth and spiritual fruit at Eddie Warrior Correctional Center. Different church groups and individuals: all a little different in doctrinal issues, but all worked together to present MERCY AND TRUTH to the wonderful, wild women at EWCC.

> **"The purpose is that through the church, the complicated, many-sided wisdom of God in all its infinite variety and innumerable aspects might now be made known..."**
> **Ephesians 3:10 (AMP)**

It is a privilege to encourage inmates to *trust* God. Many have never had someone they could trust, so it is challenging to get someone who is so wounded by those she thought she could trust to *trust* GOD. But...

> **"And He will establish you to the end keep you steadfast, give you strength and guarantee your vindication: He will be your warrant against all accusation or indictment so that you will be guiltless and irreproachable in the day of our Lord Jesus Christ. God is faithful, reliable, trustworthy, and therefore ever true to His promise, and**

He can be depended on: by Him you were called into companionship and participation with His Son, Jesus Christ our Lord.
I Corinthians 1:8,9 (AMP)

I tried to maintain a "Level of Excellence" in the chapel. Best building, most clean, best atmosphere, most organized programmatically, hardest-working chapel clerks, and most of all a spiritual level of excellence and professionalism that stretched us all: me, volunteer chaplains, chapel clerks and staff.

I wanted the female inmates at EWCC who came in darkness to go out from the facility in Light. Hope on the way in and Healing on the way out of prison. That's what we wanted when we had to fight for the right to put a steeple on the chapel. That steeple is now the first thing the inmates see when they first enter the facility.

"While you have the Light, believe in the light, have faith in it, hold to it, rely on it, that you may become sons of the Light and be filled with Light..."
John 12:36 (AMP)

I keep in touch with chapel clerks from several years back, if possible. *So many* have been successful and so badly

230

want to "give back." Many have their own businesses. Many are in paid, full-time ministry. We always hear about the ones who came back to serve another prison term. God is a God of new beginnings (more than one sometimes), but those that the volunteers and I mentored are now mentoring others. They are serving God and the changes they have made in His Name also healed their families. Many who have really *lived* the Word, have led most members of their families to the Lord. Why? Because even families (especially families) recognize that *only* God the Father, God the Son, and God the Holy Spirit can really heal and effect a change deep on the inside of a person.

Yes, incarcerated women make choices, but it is also a matter of HEALING. Only Jesus by the Power of the Holy Spirit, can go that deep into a woman's heart, mind and emotions and heal her broken heart. Remember: He said,

> **"The Spirit of the Lord is upon me because He has anointed Me, the Anointed One, the Messiah, to preach the good news, the Gospel, to the poor. He has sent Me to announce release to the captives and recovery of sight to the blind, to send forth as delivered those who are oppressed, who are downtrodden, bruised, crushed and**

> **broken down by calamity. To proclaim**
> **the accepted and acceptable year of the**
> **Lord; the day when salvation and the**
> **free favors of God profusely abound.**
> **Luke 4:18,19 (AMP)**

Sometimes, staff and security think I have made it too easy for the inmates serving their prison term. I can understand that, but as surely as some of us know really very little about the dark world they came out of; I want them to see a world different from the one they came out of.

I wanted them to experience a world that can surely be tough, but where basic courtesy, integrity, and hard work are *not only* rewarded, but are sometimes their own reward. I wanted them to experience a world where they are treated respectfully and one where they can experience true, pure joy and laughter, and feel good about themselves and others. I wanted them to experience a world of understanding where excellence and a striving to do better is an integral part of that world.

People sometimes ask how I was able to separate my ministry life from my personal life. I tried to give 110 percent as a chaplain but when I came home from EWCC, I focused on my family. And I took time off for trips with my husband and my grandsons. This brought balance to my spiritual life and kept *me* balanced. I know some ministers never take time off from their ministry because, of course, what they do is important. But I believe that balance in this area makes for a more effective minister.

I taught inmates some things and they taught *me* some things.

This is what I learned from them:

• The family you are born into can affect you negatively or positively the rest of your life.

• Relationships *can* make or break you

• Guilt and shame are crippling

• Children have a strong, *deeply* rooted love for their mothers – no matter what kind of mother they had

• Nothing is impossible with HIM

• Being Born Again is a Miracle of God

I was their Chaplain for however many years they served at Eddie Warrior, but in prison and out of prison, they will *always have a place in my heart.*

Listed below are some scriptures that I have embraced as a Chaplain. This is how I really feel about ALL the women I have had the privilege to serve who were and are at Eddie Warrior Correctional Center over two decades: the inmates who liked me as well as the ones who didn't. Even when I fell miserably short as a Chaplain so many times, the women in the prison treated me with so much respect. I couldn't help but love them.

> **"It is right and appropriate for me to have this confidence and feel this way about you all, because you have me in your heart and I hold you in my heart as partakers and sharers, one and all with me, of grace, God's unmerited favor and spiritual blessing.**
> **Philippians 1:7 AMP**
>
> **"Only God knows how much I dearly love you with the tender affection of Jesus, the Anointed One".**
> **Philippians 1:8 (TPT)**

I truly believe you if you are in a place where darkness has surrounded you or that some kind of darkness is within you; whether in prison or out of prison or never in prison, these scriptures hold true:

> **"In Him was the Life and the Life was the Light of man, And the Light shines on in the darkness and the darkness has not overpowered it..."**
> **John 1:4,5 (AMP)**

> **"Life came into being because of Him, or Life is Light for all humanity. And is Living Expression is the Light that bursts through the gloom; the Light that darkness could not diminish."**
> **John 1:4, 5 (TPT)**

> **"What came into existence was Life and the Life was Light to live by. The Life-Light blazed out of the darkness and the darkness could not put it out."**
> **John 1:5 (Message)**

I am so grateful that God sent me to prison

Amen